TWO FISH IN A TANK

HOW JOKES CAN GIVE HOPE TO OUR FRACTURED WORLD

STAY LAUGHING!

TWO FISH IN A TANK

HOW JOKES CAN GIVE HOPE TO OUR FRACTURED WORLD

ZEV BURTON

NEW DEGREE PRESS

TWO FISH IN A TANK
How Jokes Can Give Hope to Our Fractured World

ISBN   978-1-63676-801-4 *Paperback*
           978-1-63730-241-5 *Kindle Ebook*
           978-1-63730-244-6 *Ebook*

Table of Contents

To Tova and Ezri,
May you always be able to find the humor in life.
To everyone else who ever shared a laugh with me,
Thank you.

Two fish in a tank.
One says to the other,
"How the hell do you drive this thing?"

Character Flaws and Georgetown University

There is a certain horror in studying international security.

A day in the life of an international security student goes as follows: First, there is the obligatory checking of the news to answer the ever-pressing question—what has happened today that has made the world less safe? What will we be talking about in our classes today?

Most of us use Twitter for our searches. Twitter is interesting for us—there's a certain beauty to us when anyone from activists to high-level political officials have a platform to express their opinions. Through it, we are able to learn about the policies on both sides of any conflict from the sources themselves (we prefer the tweets from the foreign ministers and Secretaries of States as opposed to the CNN or Al-Jazeera summaries).

I don't follow many diplomats or state leaders on Twitter, unlike many of my peers. I prefer to keep my feed chock-full of comedians—some who are political, but many who are not.

My classmates think it's a character flaw. I beg to differ.

Humor offers insight into the world around us. There is the old adage, "it's funny because it's true," which has been backed up scientifically, and which tells us that in humor there is truth.[1] So what better way to look at the world around us than through a lens of humor?

When I asked this question to a few of my fellow classmates, their responses were akin to the following:

* Why bother with going through the added layer of political commentary when you only want the facts?

* What can a comedian tell me about the world that a reporter can't?

* Shouldn't I just go to Netflix for a chance to laugh?

In full honesty, most of us fall into one of two camps: hard power enthusiasts and soft power enthusiasts. Hard power enthusiasts see international relations as chock-full of military opportunity, where might makes right. On the other hand, soft power enthusiasts understand the importance of diplomacy and international organizations in shaping the preferences of other countries.

To be fair, my classmates and I all study at the Edmund A. Walsh School of Foreign Service at Georgetown University, a school universally known as a political and military powerhouse. Among our alumni is George Tenet, the former Director of the Central Intelligence Agency; Alexander Haig, President Ronald Reagan's Secretary of State; and Bill Clinton, the forty-second President of the United States.

---

1   Barry X. Kuhle, "It's Funny Because It's True (Because It Evokes Our Evolved Psychology)," *Review of General Psychology* 16, no. 2 (June 1, 2012): 177–186.

The Trump administration brought Georgetown alumni to the heights of foreign policy. Among our alumni: Steve Bannon, the former White House Chief Strategist and Counselor to the President; Mick Mulvaney, President Donald Trump's Chief of Staff; and Kirstjen Nielsen, the former US Secretary of Homeland Security.[2] Read: Hard power enthusiasts.

Georgetown University's required course for all International Security students is aptly titled International Security, and for decades have been teaching the next leaders of the world how military might is as important as anything else in ensuring that a country is safe from external threats. This line of thinking has gone all the way back thousands of years (which is why I've had to read various excerpts from the Peloponnesian War in nearly every class I've taken), and Georgetown upholds this tradition well.

International relations is the study of the way countries interact with each other in an inherently anarchic system. There is no overarching governing system that all countries are held to, and as such, the international system is one where countries are pretty much allowed to do whatever they want, as long as they accept the consequences.

So why would you ever follow a comedian on Twitter as opposed to a politician? This question is the central topic of this book: why should we joke in the realm of international relations, if we even should at all? Why should anyone joke about international affairs and foreign policy, perhaps some of the most serious fields there are? My

---

2   "Prominent Alumni—SFS—School of Foreign Service—Georgetown University," Georgetown University, December 11, 2020.

freshman year international relations class talked about conflict more than any other subject. It is as if conflict and war are not just pieces of the game that is international relations; they are the board the game is played on.

Put simply: it is my belief that through comedy, we create hope for the world that we live in.

There's reason to have lost hope: Populist shocks in the United States and the United Kingdom have whittled away at international institutions. We are no longer in a world defined by cooperation; rather, we are in a world where superpowers disrupt elections, tariffs and sanctions appear constantly, and conflicts in the Middle East appear never-ending.

This isn't even touching the ever-present and existential threat of climate change, or refugee crises all around the world, or terrorism, or the lack of gender equality all around the world. If you've lost hope, I understand. But there's a way to regain hope in the world: comedy.

***

Part One of this book aims to answer the pivotal question: can humor truly cross boundaries? I will argue that while some humor is inherently location- and culture-specific, there are jokes that still seem to pop up all over the world. Many of these jokes deal with corruption or politics, which signals that, while the jokes themselves may be location-dependent, the topics of the jokes are universal. We will begin to see how communities across borders are able to laugh together, even when there is no shared verbal language.

But our journey does not end there. After all, when we imagine what international relations is like, our minds conjure up images of presidents and diplomats hammering out contracts at a table. This makes sense; shows like *The West Wing* and *Scandal* portray high-profile meetings as the paramount task of politics. But to paraphrase a common phrase heard throughout the hallowed halls of Georgetown, the personal is political. In a similar manner, the political is personal—and international relations is no exception. In fact, I believe that the realm of international politics is interpersonal; that is, it's all about relationships and communications between countries and their respective people, particularly in times of extreme stress and chaos.

As such, the next two parts will discuss people and leaders. In Part Two, we will see how communities have used humor to maintain hope in the face of great oppression. In Part Three, we will explore how government officials use humor to create bonds between countries in unique but powerful ways.

And in Part Four, we will come to the realization that just because something is funny, doesn't mean it is good. We will see how humor has been used to degrade communities and advance far-right nationalism, particularly in the United States. However, we will learn how to separate humor from bigotry disguised as humor.

I hope you learn what I have learned in writing this book: that comedy and humor are essential to keeping the world hopeful, particularly in times of immense international crisis. As we will explore, jokes open us up to a world of hope—where we can hope for a better future and hope for a better life. Through hope, we can empathize for our fellow humans—or at the very least, shift our thought process away from competition and toward cooperation.

And who knows? Maybe there will be a few laughs along the way.

PART I

01

Conversations Between Stalin and Obama

——————

Ultimately, all jokes have to have three components: the setup, the punchline, and the response. The first two are the responsibility of the joke-teller, the latter belongs to the joke-listener. In telling a joke, the joker has to hope that the audience understands the joke. This doesn't always work—as a comedian myself for many years, I've learned this the hard way.

The first time I ever did comedy was in Washington, DC, just in front of a few friends at a local coffeehouse. I was nervous but excited, and I did what I could do best: make fun of my home state of Indiana.

I am from Indiana—a small town in Indiana. Anyone else from Indiana? I have asked that in Indiana and no one has clapped. We are that dumb. Like at my high school basketball games, they had to stop serving ice in the drinks because the guy who knew the recipe for ice graduated. I would say that Indiana is the spoiled yogurt of the United States, but at least spoiled yogurt has a living culture.

The joke went over well—well enough that when I came back home to Indiana, I thought that it would go amazing if I were to make the same jokes.

It didn't go over well. What worked in DC bombed in Indiana—which can teach us a lot about the location-specific nature of comedy. However, comedy appears worldwide—in fact, researchers at University College London have discovered that laughter is a universal language.[3]

Researchers at the University of Hong Kong attempt to solve this apparent paradox by stating that, "Humor is a universal phenomenon but is also culturally tinted."[4]

This does not mean that all jokes are local; rather, there must be some shared trait or experience between cultures for a joke to work across borders. At Georgetown, many students, both American and international, obsess over John Mulaney (a Hoya himself), so there must be something that we all share that can be tapped into. But what is it?

To answer this question, I sought out researcher Anastasiya Astapova, an expert in Belarusian humor. Astapova showed me a common joke told in Belarus, an Eastern European country that was formerly a part of the Soviet Union:

3   Disa A. Sauter, Frank Eisner, Paul Ekman, and Sophie K. Scott, "Cross-Cultural Recognition of Basic Emotions through Nonverbal Emotional Vocalizations," Edited by Edward E. Smith. *Proceedings of the National Academy of Sciences of the United States of America* 107, no. 6 (February 9, 2010): 2408–12.

4   Tonglin Jiang, Hao Li, and Yubo Hou, "Cultural Differences in Humor Perception, Usage, and Implications," *Frontiers in Psychology* 10 (January 29, 2019): 1–8.

Alexander Lukashenko, Hugo Chávez, and Vladimir Putin are in the boat arguing who will row.

Putin: "My country is the largest, I won't row."

Chávez: "My country is the richest in oil, I won't row."

Lukashenko: "Let's vote."

The next scene shows Putin and Chávez rowing and openly pondering: "We just cannot understand: how did we get seven votes if there are only three in the boat?"[5]

Being an international politics student, I understood the joke immediately and laughed: after all, Lukashenko (the current President of Belarus) is known to have repeatedly rigged elections to keep himself and his cronies in office. But at the core of this joke is a message about the corruption of a political leader—a message that is not unique to Belarus. In fact, I believed that I could substitute other political leaders in place of Putin, Chávez, and Lukashenko and still keep the same joke.

So, the next time I was with my friends (many of whom also study politics and are liberal), I told the following joke:

After a horrific shipwreck, Nancy Pelosi, Chuck Schumer, and Donald Trump end up in one boat. Two of them have to row, but no one wants to do it. Trump suggests a general election; the two leaders with the lowest vote counts will row. Pelosi and Schumer, both advocates of democracy, agree.

The next scene shows Pelosi and Schumer rowing while thinking, with only three in the boat, how did four vote for Trump?

---

5   Anastasiya Astapova, "Why All Dictators Have Moustaches: Political Jokes in Contemporary Belarus," *Humor* 28, no. 1 (February 3, 2015): 71–91.

Laughter ensued. As such, I became interested in what other jokes I could adapt to fit different audiences. Astapova wrote of a joke commonly told in Belarusian circles that goes as following:

Lukashenko has an argument with Bush: whose country is more democratic. Bush says, "People may go out and shout 'Bush is a fool!' in front of the White House, and they will not be punished." Lukashenko answers, "No, our country is more democratic. Everyone may go to the Residence of the President and shout 'Down with Bush!' and they will not be punished."

Here, I thought that this joke was not unique either— albeit it being about characters from several years ago. As such, I rewrote this joke as well:

Stalin is having an argument with Obama about whose countries are more democratic. Obama says, "People may go out in front of the White House and shout 'Obama is an idiot!' and they will not be punished." Stalin responds, "So? In Russia, everyone can go to Red Square and shout 'Obama is an idiot!' and will not be punished."

Once again, while the characters in the joke need to change, the joke itself follows the same format. Merely by changing protagonists and settings, the core of the joke appears to transcend national boundaries and cultures—a joke that was once Belarusian can become American fairly easily. However, there are some niche jokes that Astapova has discovered that simply do not translate from one culture to another: language jokes and puns. This makes intuitive sense, as puns tend to only work in one language due to language constraints. (After sending this out to a few friends, I was made aware of one exception: the joke "Q: Where do cats go after they die? A: Purrrr-gatory," when translated into Spanish still works, albeit in a different way: "Q: ¿Dónde van los gatos después de la muerte? A: Pur-gato-rio.")

The quick and easy retort to this is the same that many in older generations like to make: life isn't all online and on the Internet; what about when it comes to face-to-face interaction? All around the world, people speak different languages and have different customs—how is humor going to suddenly transcend all of those differences?

Welcome to the island of Taquile. The island of Taquile is just over two square miles on the Peruvian side of Lake Titicaca. Known for their fine handwoven textiles and hospitality, the inhabitants of Taquile are known as Taquileños. Taquileños speak Puno Quechua, a dialect of the Southern Quechua language.

Lexi Castro is a good friend of mine—we met in a class titled "Political Violence in the Name of God." As a brief but interesting aside, that class had fifteen female students and two male students (as is somewhat typical in soft-power classes, for reasons that could fill a shelf in a library, so I'll leave it to you to speculate why this is). She doesn't speak Puno Quechua, but she was staying with the Taquileños and had to figure out a way to bond with them. A few days into her visit, Castro started making funny faces at the kids ("kinda like peekaboo"). The kids would run over to her, hug her, and she'd pretend to fall over. Then the adults began to make some of her faces back at her, with everyone laughing. "Anytime the little kids touched me, I fell over, and anytime I touched them, they'd fall over laughing. The adults got in on it and started fake falling over too." Even though Castro and the Taquileños had no language similarities, comedy brought them together. Castro recalls playing with a young child by the name of Evé, who only spoke Puno Quechua. Regardless of this language barrier, they still played together every day.

As Castro recalls, "By playing and joking around, these kids bridged this huge gap that made us all so comfortable around each other even when we couldn't speak a single word to each other."

Humor literally transcended all of these differences—whether it was culture, language, or any other difference, comedy brought Castro and the Taquileños together.

Castro's story leads to an interesting question—are words even necessary for humor to bring people together?

One of the most popular forms of comedy on the internet is that of the home video, the slapstick-based videos that capture individuals in embarrassing or surprising situations, like a man slipping on a banana peel. These videos were popular all over the world before the rise of the internet—the United States has a show about it (*America's Funniest Home Videos*), and so do the United Kingdom (*You've Been Framed*) and Israel (*Fisfusim*).

Presumably, this fact is because home videos are personal—due to the bottom-up nature of the internet, anyone and everyone can make and share these videos. A similar explanation can be given to the preponderance of photo-based humor on the Internet. Another reason is that these videos are remarkably short; as a result, they are easier to share and circulate via e-mail or online. The third and final possible explanation is the most interesting: the kinds of humor that these jokes are based on, that is physical, visual, childish, and slapstick humor, is not culture-specific by any means. No matter what country or region you come from, a man slipping on a banana peel is hilarious.

But is this a phenomenon that we actually see? Do we see similar jokes all over the world (and not just when a student like myself actively adapts them for their own research)?

Our answer lies within the same place that many of you spend countless hours on: the internet.

02

Make Sure He's Dead

The internet is a boundless place, chock-full of anything from Cincinnati Reds scores to breadstick recipes to men who are just a little too into *My Little Pony*.

But, as humans, when we have the totality of information at our fingertips, when we have the computational power that got man to the moon in our pockets, we choose to make jokes.

This isn't a complaint—in fact, these very jokes are the focus of this chapter. Because such jokes can travel across national boundaries within milliseconds; what a mother in Denmark writes on her Facebook wall can be read by her son in New York City within a matter of seconds. The same goes for jokes.

Jokes in the internet are unique—unlike person-to-person comedy, jokes are purely textual; that is, there is no vocal variation or timing involved. As a result, any joke destined to spread on the internet must be funny at face value. There is no shortage of these jokes—countless websites are dedicated to humor and jokes, including personal blogs that provide funny analysis of contemporary events to professional humor websites (e.g. The Onion). Limor Shifman of the University of Oxford calls these websites "humor hubs," a term I will employ to refer to them as well. A humor hub is a "large, dynamic repository of visual and verbal humor about various topics."[6]

Shifman's amazing study took a look at all of these humor hubs to answer the simple question: what jokes make it on the internet, and what jokes don't? In analyzing hundreds of jokes for their topic, their incongruity, and 'their butt' (the target of the mockery within the joke, and also the best variable name of all time), he was able to come up with the top most joked-about topics—let's look at the top twelve:

1. Sex

2. Gender

3. Animals

4. Product/Company

5. Mass Media

6. Children/Teenagers

7. Politics

8. Computers/Technology

9. Sports

10. Specific People

11. Ethnicity

12. Transportation

---

6   Limor Shifman, "Humor in the Age of Digital Reproduction: Continuity and Change in Internet-Based Comic Texts," *International Journal of Communication* 1 (2007): 187–209.

It makes sense why sex-based jokes are at the top of the list—sex is undertaken and understood by every society and nation in the world. Perhaps more than anything else, sex is a global topic. This also explains why gender is second on the list, since nearly every society has them (and as such, relations between the genders that serve as fodder for joking).

Turning to animal humor's prevalence on the internet, the reasoning may be due to the basic incongruities that underlay the humor. Most of the jokes involve some sort of incongruity between humans and non-human animals (animals that behave or look like humans). Once again, we see the globally-oriented aspects of humor on the internet—the human traits that the animals appear to imitate are universal. Another potential explanation comes from the ancient fable—how internet jokes are the modern-day fables. Like internet animal jokes, fables usually have animals behaving as humans, fables are universal, and in many cases, their original author is unknown. Every culture has their version of fables; the difference between fables and internet humor is that, where fables tell us what is right and what is wrong, internet animal jokes are usually non-political. Therefore, these jokes can be transferred all around the world with little to no manipulation.

The first three most popular topics (sex, gender, and animals) are inherently globally-oriented, since all social groups are aware of them. In contrast, localized jokes such as politics and sports appear much less frequently (places seven and nine, respectively). This makes intuitive sense—while jokes about Mexicans may thrive in places like the United States, countries such as Israel or Namibia would not gain as much pleasure from hearing such a joke. The lack of ethnically-based humor reinforces the idea of the global prevailing over the local on the internet.

From this analysis, we can see that while humor is culture-dependent, there are similarities across every culture, such as sex, gender relations, and animals, that serve as unifiers. Jokes about sex, gender, and age deal with social categories common to societies all over the world. This isn't to say that jokes on these topics have the same message or underlying truth in every culture, just that they are based on universal categories (young/old, for instance). Contrasting these categories of jokes are the three other domains of joking: language, politics, and ethnicity, which tend to draw more heavily on locality and culture.

While interesting, Shifman's analysis is not the only way we can determine how jokes are universal. In 2001, the British Science Association partnered with University of Hertfordshire Psychology professor Richard Wiseman, host of the popular YouTube channel *Quirkology*. The question they sought out to answer was simple: What is the world's funniest joke?

Thus, LaughLab was born. The project had two sections. First, people could submit their own jokes. Second, people could rate how funny they found randomly suggested jokes from the first part. When it came to rating the jokes, Wiseman believed that he found the world's funniest joke with higher ratings than any other. Drum roll please...

A couple of New Jersey hunters are out in the woods when one of them falls to the ground. He doesn't seem to be breathing, his eyes are rolled back in his head. The other guy whips out his cell phone and calls the emergency services. He gasps to the operator: "My friend is dead! What can I do?" The operator, in a calm, soothing voice says: "Just take it easy. I can help. First, let's make sure he's dead." There is a silence, then a shot is heard. The guy's voice comes back on the line. He says: "Okay, now what?"

The joke worked across many different countries, cultures, and demographics for a multitude of reasons. Wiseman offers his own thoughts on why this joke won, stating how jokes "sometimes make us feel superior to others, reduce the emotional impact of anxiety-provoking situations, or surprise us because of some kind of incongruity. The hunters joke contains all three elements—we feel superior to the stupid hunter, realize the incongruity of him misunderstanding the operator, and the joke helps us to laugh about our concerns about our own mortality."[7]

The winning joke was not submitted by a comedian, as I expected it to be. Rather, it was thirty-one-year-old UK-based psychiatrist Gurpal Gosall who submitted the joke. When Wiseman asked him why he liked the joke so much, Gosall told Wiseman, "I like the joke as it makes people feel better, because it reminds them that there is always someone out there who is doing something more stupid than themselves." For a psychiatrist, he would often tell that joke to his patients because it helped them cope with their experiences.

Gosall's thoughts lead us directly to our next section, where we will explore how jokes are used to cope in the face of tragedy.

---

7   Richard Wiseman, "LaughLab: The Scientific Search for the World's Funniest Joke," LaughLab, October 3, 2002.

PART II

03

Taliban Bingo

———

There was a comedian, whose name I have forgotten, that came to my middle school to talk to us about bullying one day. We were jerks to each other—as middle schoolers are. But this comedian had a solution: if we were being bullied, we should respond with a compliment in an aggressive manner.

Needless to say, we made fun of this (and him) for the remainder of the school year and beyond. Echoes of "You (sic)" were followed by "Yeah? Well, I really like your shoes today!"

There's a certain irony in making fun of this strategy—but when some people decided to try it out in practice, it was funny and disarming. For those who were on the receiving end of such insults, humor became a way to both cope with the insults and disarm the bullies. It's a small glimpse into the world of humor in battle—and I believe it's a microcosm of the international system at play.

In the second part of this book, we are going to take our time exploring how the people of a nation used humor in order to cope with, and then resist, forces that wished them dead. We will see repeatedly the idea of hope—that humor gave them hope when the world was crumbling around them. While I may study war and conflict, I see that the use of humor to cope is not limited to activity in war; in fact, other threats such as fascism or pandemics also give way to comedy.

As you read this section, I want you to follow the journey that happens over and over again—first we cope, then we find hope, and then we resist. We will see how nations come together to cope, to laugh, and then to fight for justice.

Just to be clear, when I say 'nation,' this does not automatically mean a country. Rather, I'll be using the definition provided to us by the great Cornell political scientist Benedict Anderson:

[A nation] is an imagined political community—and imagined as both inherently limited and sovereign.[8]

It is imagined because not every member of the nation will know each other, limited because the nation is finite in size (as it is impossible to have an infinite number of individuals in a group), sovereign as it has some level of freedom, and a community as those within the nation see themselves as in a "deep, horizontal comradeship."[9] Juxtapose this to the idea of a country—while the United States or France or Libya may be both a nation and a country, the Kurds in Turkey believe that they belong to a Kurdish nation and the Jewish diaspora believe that they belong to a Jewish nation.

---

8   Benedict Anderson, *Imagined Communities: Reflections on the Origin and Spread of Nationalism.* (London: Verso, 2016).

9   Ibid.

With this in mind, let's explore how a nation copes during tragedies with humor.

Humor prevents us from emotionally threatening situations—such as a terrorist attack on a major city—by reducing the experience of stressful stimuli. William Kahn, a professor of organizational behavior at Boston University, summarizes that "[humor] is a serious act of coping, performed humorously."[10] Think about workers making fun of their job with each other, and you begin to see how this works on a larger scale than one individual. When multiple people all joke about the same topics, they form connections that allow them to cope with effects collectively. These interpersonal connections are the way that negative emotions such as anxiety or fear can be shared and expressed. Humor as a coping mechanism is backed empirically as well: in 2011, Stanford psychologists discovered that people who recovered the best from negative situations used humor to cope with the circumstances in a positive light.[11]

But as we talked about before, humor is a form of messaging—requiring both a joke-teller and a joke-listener. Both by delivering and receiving messages in a humorous manner, individuals are able to communicate in ambiguous ways. In some scenarios, ambiguity is a flaw; in humor, it is an asset. This ambiguity is often what makes a joke funny. Think about the joke from last chapter about the man shooting his friend. When we laugh at that joke,

---

10   William A. Kahn, "To Wit: Humor and Applied Behavioral Science," *The Journal of Applied Behavioral Science* 26, no. 3 (August 1, 1990): 329–30.

11   Max McClure, "Stanford Psychologists Find That Jokes Help Us Cope with Horrifying Images," Stanford News Release, Stanford University, August 1, 2011.

we think, "Of course that's not what the 911 operator meant, you silly goose!"

On another level, humor enables individuals to reframe their worldview in the face of adversity. Humor allows individuals to step back psychologically and see a situation differently than they typically would. This makes intuitive sense—humor inherently challenges the "normal" at almost no cost or risk. As a society, humor allows for reframing national and global conversations. Jokes allow for a nation to acknowledge the existence of various threats without directly stating them aloud— through a joke, reality enters into the mindset of a nation without the threat fully becoming realized. The joke acts as a buffer, a bit like adding some sugar to help the medicine go down.

As our example of a nation working together to cope with a tragedy, let's take a look at how the satirical newspaper The Onion turned to humor after the events of 9/11—and more importantly, how coping Americans responded to the humor.

The Onion is known for articles such as "Congress Passes Americans With No Abilities Act" and "Kim Jong-Un Named The Onion's Sexiest Man Alive For 2012" (the latter of which the largest newspaper in China actually used as a source for one of their articles).[12] On September 10, 2001, employees of The Onion gathered for a party, full of whiskey and proposals. The Onion's first New York issue was due to be published the next day, and the world, to them, was theirs.

---

12   Scott Simon, "Sexiest Man Alive Gets 'The Onion' Taken Seriously," NPR, December 1, 2012.

The next day, writers watched as the events of September 11 unfolded before their eyes. The September 11 issue never made it to print.

During the September 11 attacks of 2001, almost three thousand people died and more than six thousand were injured by the hijacked planes crashing into the World Trade Centers and the Pentagon.[13] Much of the drama was played out live on national television, including the crash of the second plane into the South Tower at 9:03 a.m. and both towers collapse just over an hour later. One study found that it is the most memorable moment shared by US TV viewers in the last fifty years.[14]

As of writing, the attacks are the deadliest terrorist act in world history. For the United States, the attacks were the most devastating incident since the attack on Pearl Harbor almost sixty years earlier.

Citizens from more than ninety countries were victims, including the United Kingdom (sixty-seven deaths), the Dominican Republic (forty-seven) and India (forty-one).[15]

The attacks sparked many dramatic impacts all around the world, such as ongoing wars in Afghanistan and Iraq, the establishment of the Department of Homeland Security that merged and formed twenty-two government offices such as the US Immigration and Customs Enforcement office, and the booming of the US intelligence state

13 Brad Plumer, "Nine Facts about Terrorism in the United States since 9/11," *The Washington Post,* September 11, 2013.

14 Post Staff Report, "Sept. 11 Attack Most Memorable TV Moment from Past 50 Years," *New York Post*, August 27, 2013.

15 Carolee Walker, "America.gov—Telling America's Story—Five-Year 9/11 Remembrance Honors Victims from 90 Countries", America. gov, September 11, 2006.

with the USA Patriot Act.[16] Nearly every American still is impacted by the 9/11 attacks and the American responses.

One week later, the staff gathered at The Onion's offices on 20th Street, just over a mile's walk from the 9/11 rubble. "It was a terrible meeting," the longtime writer John Krewson recalled. "We knew we wouldn't be able to ignore what had happened, but it was hard to make any sort of comedy."

Eventually, one staffer said that American life had become "a bad Jerry Bruckheimer movie."

Head writer Carol Kolb pushed the metaphorical ball of comedy more, writing the headline, "Not Knowing What Else To Do, Woman Bakes American-Flag Cake."

Krewson recalled that the headline "was poignant. It captured how stunned and confused everyone was at the time."

More and more headlines followed:

U.S. Vows to Defeat Whoever It Is We're At War With

Hijackers Surprised To Find Selves in Hell: 'We Expected Eternal Paradise for This,' Say Suicide Bombers

God Angrily Clarifies 'Don't Kill' Rule

Rest of Country Temporarily Feels Deep Affection for New York

Hugging Up 76,000 Percent

The Onion's issue was slowly, but surely, coming together in the form of these headlines. The staff, worried about making jokes so soon after the worst terrorist attack ever

---

16   History.com Editors, "September 11 Attacks," History.com, A&E Television Networks, February 17, 2010.

on America, thought that it was going to be the worst issue of The Onion—and perhaps their last one ever.

The issue was printed on September 26, just fifteen days after the attacks that crippled the nation.

When writers arrived the next day at the office, the fax machine was overflowing with comments from readers.

"The top one just read, 'That's funny, that's funny, that's funny,'" Krewson recalled.

However, Krewson believes that the comedy wasn't pristine, perfectly-written comedy. "It wasn't an especially funny issue. In fact, I'd say it was the least funny issue we've ever done, but it was cathartic."[17, 18]

However, the Onion writers were not the only one making jokes. In fact, they weren't even the first.

The first joke surfaced online on 9/11, just under two hours after the first tower fell:

Q: What does WTC stand for?

A: What Trade Center?

A: Welcome to Canada.

A: World Terrorist Center.[19]

American studies scholar Bill Ellis spent the months after the attack charting and analyzing the jokes that swirled

17 "Remembering The Onion's 9/11 Issue: 'Everyone Thought This Would Be Our Last Issue in Print'." Yahoo! News, Yahoo!, August 25, 2011.

18 The Onion, "American Life Turns Into Bad Jerry Bruckheimer Movie," *The Onion*, October 18, 2017.

19 Amanda Hess, "Why Teenagers Love Making Jokes About 9/11," *Slate Magazine*, July 6, 2015.

03 TALIBAN BINGO · 39

around the internet, leading to some interesting results.[20] On September 17, a list of forty-five jokes, plus a "top ten" list of "good things about the WTC attack," began to spread on numerous message boards and e-mail lists such as 4Chan and Reddit. These jokes were spread fairly conservatively around the internet, mostly resonating on message boards dedicated to dark humor. Many were recycled jokes from previous disasters, such as the Challenger explosion of 1986:

Q: What color were the pilot's eyes?

A: Blue. One blew this way and the other blew that way.

The next day, visual jokes began to populate the internet. Most notably, reconstructions of the World Trade Center as four towers to form the obscene gesture of giving the middle finger. One caption to such a reconstruction read simply, "Rebuilding New York's Skyline. New Trade Center design incorporates a gesture and spirit familiar to all New Yorkers."

Two days after that, a letter circulated around the internet and e-mail chains, challenging the Taliban to "an old-fashioned game of Whoop-ass." The full text is below:

Dear Taliban, Mr. bin Laden, Mr. Arafat, and Mr. Hussein, et al:

We are pleased to announce that we unequivocally accept your challenge to an old-fashioned game of Whoop-ass. Now that we understand the rule that there are no rules, we look forward to playing without them for the first time. Since this game is winner-take-all, we unfortunately will be unable to invite you

---

20   Bill Ellis, "Making A Big Apple Crumble: The Role of Humor in Constructing a Global Response to Disaster," *New Directions in Folklore*, no. 6 (June 6, 2002): 35–80.

to join us at the victory celebration. But rest assured that we will toast you—LITERALLY.

While we will admit that you are off to an impressive lead, it is, however, now our turn at the plate. By the way, we will be playing on your diamond now…Batter up!

Our team lineup is as follows:

Co-owners—The FATHER, SON, and HOLY GHOST

Manager—George W. Bush

Asst. Manager—Dick Cheney

Head Coach—Colin Powell

Asst. Coach—Donald Rumsfeld

Starting Pitcher—Norman Schwarzkopf

1ˢᵗ Base—US Marine Corps

2ⁿᵈ Base—US Navy

3ʳᵈ Base—US Air Force

Shortstop and Cleanup hitter—US Army

Outfield—Firemen and Policemen

Umpire—None required *

remember—the manager told you there'll be no discussion; no negotiation; and you didn't want rules, anyway!

Pinch hitters as needed—

US Navy Seals

US Army Green Berets

US Army Rangers

US Air Force PJs

Delta Force

And, since there are no rules, we've decided to add:

4th Base—United Kingdom

5th Base—Russia

6th Base—China

Other Bases (as desired)—Pakistan, Japan, Germany. France, Spain, Italy, Israel, Saudi Arabia, Egypt, Turkistan, lots of other...Stans, and more.

Opening ceremonies:

Vocal 1: Celine Dion—"The Star-Spangled Banner"

Vocal 2: Lee Greenwood—"God Bless the U.S.A."

Vocal 3: Bruce Springsteen—"Born in the U.S.A."

Vocal 4: The Mormon Tabernacle Choir—"Battle Hymn of the Republic"

You may choose whoever you want for your team...it won't really matter (even if you all shave), our guys are gonna win!

Sincerely,

On behalf of the 270 million citizens of the United States of America

p.s. May we recommend at this time that you give your soul to Allah; because your butt is OURS!!!!! Goodbye, literally.[21]

Other long-form jokes, such as a falsified speech from President George W. Bush saying that "Afghanistan will end up a giant kitty litter box," took the internet by storm. A fake weather report stated that "the five-day forecast for Afghanistan is two days," an adaption of a

---

21   Giselinde Kuipers, "'Where Was King Kong When We Needed Him?' Public Discourse, Digital Disaster Jokes, and the Functions of Laughter after 9/11." *The Journal of American Culture* 28, no. 1 (February 9, 2005): 70–84.

joke typically associated with the 1979 Three-Mile Island Nuclear Plant mishap in Pennsylvania. [22, 23]

At the same time, all the way across the pond, British individuals were injecting their own humor into the mix. One particular joke gained traction all throughout the country:

Q: Why is the USA the only country where miracles come true?

A: Because it's the only country with a four-sided Pentagon.

Once President Bush began military action in Afghanistan, a new wave of jokes emerged, mostly concerning the war itself:

Q: How do you play Taliban bingo?

A: B-52 F-16 B-1 etc.

Q: What is the difference between Christmas and the Taliban?

A: Christmas will be there in December.

Some jokes suggested both the coming revenge on the Taliban but also on the catastrophic event that started it all:

Q: How is bin Laden like Fred Flintstone?

A: Both may look out their windows and see Rubble.

These jokes, Ellis theorized, worked by "calling into consciousness the key images of the media disaster, then immediately projecting them onto the scapegoat bin Laden."[24]

These are not objectively funny jokes, nor are they the pinnacle of comedy by any stretch of the imagination.

---

22   Ibid.

23   Mikita Brottman, "What's So Funny About 9/11?" *The Chronicle of Higher Education*, February 12, 2012.

24   Ellis, "Making a Big Apple Crumble," *New Directions in Folklore*.

As such, the question becomes: What function did this dark humor serve?

There are two reasons why this is the case.

Our first answer is relatively simple, and was summarized succinctly by one commenter: "If you don't laugh, you'll cry."

Take a look at what was going around in the field of technology in 2001 and we begin to see why jokes proliferated at such an astonishing rate. As technology and television brought previously obscure national events into homes all over the world, everyone suddenly needed their own coping mechanism. As newscasters continued to run footage of either the catastrophe itself or Ground Zero, jokes helped surface the very real and very complicated feelings that arose after a surreal and commercialized national disaster. Even the British, though they were distanced geographically and culturally from Americans, used jokes to both support their ally and themselves in this uncertain time.

Our second answer is a little more violent: the jokes almost all come with the promise of violence/death/war. In a way, politicians could have (and should have) looked to these jokes to understand how Americans were reacting to the tragedy. It allowed for Americans to say that they wanted revenge without sounding like bloodthirsty animals.

For a nation coping with the greatest terror attack on American soil, humor allowed them to, if just for a moment, be relieved on the tension and fear building up inside of them—in many cases, this includes redirecting that tension toward the enemy. Humor let them feel hopeful that their country would survive such an attack.

***

Sociologist Antonin Obrdlik uses the word *galgenhu-mor* to describe gallows humor; that is, humor that is expressly making fun of an otherwise terrifying situation. Gallows humor is grim and ironic—in a world where you are terrified for your life, it makes absolutely no sense to make jokes.[25]

But that's precisely what sometimes happens.

Take Czechoslovakia during the Second World War. After the Munich Pact in 1938, the region in the north of Czechoslovakia became part of the Greater German Reich. Soon after, Adolf Hitler invaded the rest of the country and declared in 1939 a new state: the Protectorate of Bohemia and Moravia.

At the beginning of the Second World War, over 350 thousand Jews lived in the area. At the end of it, only fourteen thousand remained.

This seems like the least likely time to joke. But this is exactly when gallows humor came to light.

Antonin Obrdlik, himself having lived through this oppression, has a theory as to why this happened:

People who live in absolute uncertainty as to their lives and property find a refuge in inventing, repeating, and spreading through the channels of whispering counter-propaganda, anecdotes, and jokes about their oppressors. This is gallows humor at its best because it originates and functions among people

25   Antonin J. Obrdlik, "'Gallows Humor'-A Sociological Phenomenon," *American Journal of Sociology* 47, no. 5 (March 1942): 709–16.

who literally face death at any moment. Some of them even dare to collect the jokes as philatelists collect stamps.

Why did this occur? Simply put, the oppressed had to strengthen their hope, otherwise they would not be able to survive with their grave situation. The impact of gallows humor was enormous—Odbrdlik recalls how one good joke would change pessimists into optimists. Without galgenhumor in Czechoslovakia, the oppressed would have lost all hope.

We know that the horrors of the Holocaust were not just limited to those in Czechoslovakia. Despite this (or perhaps because of it), in the ghettos and concentration and death camps, there were humor and laughter. Jews stuck within camps, awaiting their deaths, were hopeless and could not resist—if they did, they disappeared forever.

Jokes safeguard our emotional and physical health from reality when reality is too much to bear. When we perceive humorous elements in negative situations, we gain a new perspective, thus avoiding the full impact of such negative situations. The coping experienced was individual, but since every individual in the concentration camps experienced it, humor became the lubricant for social interaction and created as positive an atmosphere as possible. For example, many jokes were harsh, brazen, and offensive—a situation funny to veteran prisoners was terrifying to new prisoners, signaling that the long-term prisoners had adapted to the camps' brutality. From the funny stories the old-timers told, newcomers could derive information on how to survive, what the societal norms were, and how to accept their new reality.

Chaya Ostrower, author of *It Kept Us Alive: Humor in the Holocaust*, notes how "this was the educational, didactic function of humor in the camp; a successful joke could replace long explanations and illustrate the situation better than relating numerous details." As some German Jews used to quip, "How many types of Jews are there? Two: optimists and pessimists. All the pessimists are in exile, and the optimists are in concentration camps."[26]

Adolf Hitler, the leader of the German Nazi party, was not too fond of comedy. In fact, there is proof that Hitler had a unique horror at being laughed at because he banned any anti-Nazi jokes. Jokes were considered acts of treason (some people even were put on trial for naming their pets "Adolf"). Performers in cabaret shows were forced into exile if not killed, and some were even put in concentration camps. As a result, the cabaret went from the stage to the camps.

The Night of Blood on the Rock of Horrors or Knight Adolar's Maiden Voyage and Its Gruesome End or That is Not True Love was one written by Rudolf Kalmar and performed within the camps. Kalmar wrote the play on scraps of discarded paper around the camp. He called his play, which was designed to make inmates laugh through anti-Nazi jokes and impersonations of Hitler, "a parable of the small spirit of the great Reich." The play ended with the following lines:

It is the old song,

That you see here in this play.

But always keep a word in mind:

---

26   Rudolph Herzog and Jefferson Chase, *Dead Funny: Telling Jokes in Hitler's Germany.* (Brooklyn, NY, New York: Melville House, 2012).

Everything is hell,

Soon it will get well

Through this magic word: humor, humor![27]

The nation of Jews in concentration camps needed hope. And through humor, they got closer to it.

---

27   Whitney Carpenter, "Laughter in a Time of Tragedy: Examining Humor during the Holocaust," *Denison Journal of Religion* 9 (2010): 12–25.

04

Judas, You On?

But let's take this a step further: are there examples where comedy is used against an existential threat? To be fair, this book so far has been covering humor in times of conflict (World War II). However, this does not mean that the benefits of humor in international relations should be limited to merely conflict—for example, the global issue of climate change, one of the direr threats to the human race as a whole, is a place where comedy should be encouraged.

This concept appears counterintuitive, as climate change has caused myriads of environmental, migratory, and human rights issues that could take up an entire library, let alone a single publication. The fear of climate change has sparked a new term: eco-anxiety, which the American Psychological Association defined as the "chronic fear of environmental doom."[28] Eco-anxiety stems from the depression and anxiety that people can't do anything to stop climate change from occurring. Like the

---

28 "Climate Change's Toll On Mental Health," *American Psychological Association*, March 29, 2017. American Psychological Association.

battlefield of war, the battlefield of climate change is not good fodder for comedy.

Or is it? Recent research has been hinting that the power of humor to combat eco-anxiety goes beyond just temporary distraction. A team of researchers have published several papers as to how comedy can influence the way we feel about climate change. This team is led by University of Colorado Professor Beth Osnes, who has toured with her original musical *Shine* to teach youth voices on energy and climate. First, they had students participate in a number of comedy workshops related to climate change, including coming up with their own skits (and if you've ever watched college students come up with their own skits, the image itself is humorous).[29]

After the workshops, 90 percent of the students said they felt more hopeful about climate change. Perhaps more importantly, 83 percent of participants said that they felt their commitment to taking action on climate change was stronger and more likely to last. It appears that, as the researchers concluded, that comedy helps people "positively process negative emotions regarding global warming" and "sustain hope."[30] Comedy helps us positively work through these emotions.

The one major flaw in this study is that the participants only felt like their commitment to climate change activism would last—but would it actually last? While they may have felt inspired to take action when they came home from the testing room, what was going to happen

---

29   Beth Osnes, Maxwell Boykoff, and Patrick Chandler, "Good-Natured Comedy to Enrich Climate Communication," *Comedy Studies* 10, no. 2 (June 3, 2019): 224–36.

30   Ibid.

in a year? Or three years? Would people remain inspired, or would their willingness to commit to climate change action fizzle out over time?

Fortunately, our heroes at the University of Colorado Boulder asked the same question. They analyzed a series of stand-up shows at the university called *Stand Up for Climate Change* and tracked how the audience responded over the three years after the series.

The researchers concluded that "while science is often privileged as the dominant way by which climate change is articulated, comedic approaches can influence how meanings course through the veins of our social body, shaping our coping and survival practices in contemporary life."[31] Point being: comedy makes people more aware of climate change, brings an emotional element to the conversation, and makes the audience think about solutions.

Take comedian Ilana Glazer's special, aptly titled *The Planet is Burning*, named to get the word out about climate change. As she would tell Trevor Noah on *The Daily Show*, "The planet is burning and we're not talking about it all the time. It's like, pathetically funny." Noah responded, "If I was going to have billboards and repeat a phrase over and over, this is probably a worthwhile one." It's "free climate change advertising."[32]

In 2018, the Intergovernmental Panel on Climate Change warned that the world only had until about 2030 to take steps that could limit global warming to manageable

---

31   Maxwell Boykoff and Beth Osnes, "A Laughing Matter? Confronting Climate Change through Humor," *Political Geography* 68 (2019): 154–63.

32   Episode, *The Daily Show with Trevor Noah* 25, no. 54, January 28, 2020.

levels.[33] Trevor Noah observed, "You know the crazy people you see in the streets shouting that the world is ending? Turns out, they're all actually climate scientists."[34]

Another example comes to mind when we discuss war against a non-human enemy: pandemics. More specifically, the coronavirus pandemic of 2020.

Few years in history were like 2020. Plagued by a literal plague, millions of people were under lockdown, prevented from ever leaving their house except for bare necessities—and even then, they had to wear a mask to prevent the spread of the novel coronavirus. People were stuck with nothing but an internet connection and pets. Millions of people died.[35]

So naturally, there were jokes made about the entire situation. One tweet read, "Unreasonably dark joke, but shouldn't we wait until after the pandemic to fill out the [2020] US census?"[36]

The joke itself is dark—but it's not unique by any means. As the pandemic ravaged the world, the internet was flush with coronavirus-related jokes and memes. Twitter quips came a dime a dozen. "A year from now, you'll all be laughing about this virus," reads one tweet. "Not all of you, obviously."[37]

33   "Summary for Policymakers of IPCC Special Report on Global Warming of 1.5°C Approved by Governments," *The Intergovernmental Panel on Climate Change*, October 8, 2018, United Nations.

34   Episode, *The Daily Show*, 2020.

35   COVID-19 Dashboard, Baltimore, Maryland: Johns Hopkins University, 2021.

36   Alex Williams, "It's OK to Find Humor in Some of This," *The New York Times*, April 22, 2020.

37   Ibid.

On TikTok, the viral video-sharing app, it seemed like every other post that I scrolled through was making a joke about the coronavirus. Even in December, ten months after the March 2020 lockdown period, there were still jokes being made on the platform about the pandemic and how it was impacting everyday life.

Humor has always played a role in dark times as a shared psychological release between all members of a society, or in this case, the world. There is a German word for this (because of course there is): *welschmertz. Welschmertz* is that mood of sentimental sadness at the state of inadequacy or imperfection of the world compared to the ideal state. Joachim Whaley, a professor of German history and thought at the University of Cambridge, describes it as "pain suffered simultaneously both in the world and at the state of the world, with the sense that the two are linked."[38] It is sadness at the world over something we cannot control, like a global pandemic.

With so little contact with others, save the few people we quarantined with, our jokes are akin to an SOS message, as if we are saying, "Is anyone else out here struggling or is it just me?" When we receive the likes or the retweets or the comments, we know that we are all going through this together—which makes the experience of being under quarantine slightly more bearable. Some of the jokes are tasteless like the ones above; others are silly, like showing Jesus conducting the Last Supper via the videoconferencing app Zoom (with the epic line, "Judas, you on?"). They provide a fleeting distraction as

---

38   Jill Petzinger and Marta Cooper, "There's a German Word People Use in Times of Despair, and It's as Apt Today as It Was in the 19th Century," Quartz, October 18, 2016.

the pandemic put so many lives on hold. Lori Day, an educational psychologist, described the experience as "very similar to the feeling I get looking at baby animals online, which is another thing I dose myself liberally with these days." Day runs a private Facebook group dedicated to coronavirus-related jokes. Some members of the group are ill with the virus, but they still laugh. "They're thanking me from their beds," Day said. "They're thanking me from their hospital rooms."[39]

The prominent forms of jokes are mostly punching up at authorities and politicians; however, some jokes have been directed toward the virus itself. We will take those one by one. As late-night hosts such as Trevor Noah, Steven Colbert, and John Oliver have shown, it is easy to mock the politicians who prioritize votes and the economy over lives. Seth Meyers, host of *Late Night with Seth Meyers*, noted how minutes before the President of the United States was supposed to address a troubled nation, 2008 Vice Presidential Nominee and former Governor of Alaska Sarah Palin appeared on the show *The Masked Singer*, singing Sir Mix-a-Lot's "Baby Got Back." (As Meyer's said, "It was so depressing, Sir Mix-a-Lot immediately wrote a sequel called "Baby Got Prozac."") US President Donald Trump addressed the nation and, when the broadcast failed to cut after the speech, let out an exasperated, "Okay." Meyers, punching up at the president, pounced on the opportunity to critique the address, saying that:

[Trump] reacted to his speech the way the rest of us reacted to it; "Okay, that was weird." It's like if [Former US President Franklin Delano Roosevelt] had said, "Yesterday, December 7, a day which will live in infamy, the United States was suddenly

39   Williams, "It's OK," 2020.

and deliberately attacked by naval and air forces of the Empire of Japan, so, like, that just happened!"[40]

For many Americans, Trump messed up the coronavirus response, and Meyer's joke gave them a chance to laugh at their president. One similar-themed meme reads, "Calm down everyone, a six-time bankrupted reality TV star is handling the situation."[41] These jokes serve a valuable purpose: to keep spirits high and hold those in power accountable.

On the other hand, jokes have been directed toward the coronavirus. On the dating app Tinder, a profile for "Coronavirus, 29" has the bio of "I love being outdoors, crowded places, and food markets." Other jokes poke fun at the similar-named beer brand Corona ("What goes well with the coronavirus? Lyme disease"). Coronavirus doesn't care about whether you joke about it or not; those who joke about coronavirus aren't any more likely to become infected than those who don't. So, we might as well joke about it, for our own sake!

These jokes include poking fun at the national quarantines everyone faces. Stephen Colbert, host of *The Late Show with Stephen Colbert*, did one of his nightly shows dressed in the top half of a suit while submerged in a bubble bath at home ("I've been avoiding human contact since before it was cool.").[42] Once again, poking fun

---

40 Seth Meyers, "Trump Addresses the Nation on the Coronavirus Pandemic: A Closer Look," YouTube video, 16:35, March 12, 2020.

41 Unsubscribe Memes, 2020, "Calm down everyone," Facebook, March 23, 2020.

42 Stephen Colbert, "The Big Story Tonight Is YOU—A Special "Social Distancing" Edition Of The Late Show," YouTube Video, 10:34, March 17, 2020.

04 JUDAS, YOU ON? · 55

at quarantining doesn't attack any individual or group, but provides a necessary release from the unique situation millions have found themselves within. It's validating—what others are going through is the same as what I'm going through. It's knowing that other people are, while apart physically, going through the same reality emotionally.

On the other hand, making jokes of difficult situations allows us to come face to face with the very real situations that people find themselves in. It's hard to have a difficult conversation about climate change or a pandemic without being at least a little bit uncomfortable, which is where humor comes in. Humor adds a little bit of sugar to the medicine, making it easier to stomach the state of the world we live in, both with conflict and without.

Because at the end of the day, it doesn't matter if people are hopeless because of a conflict or hopeless because of a global pandemic—people are still without hope. While comedy and humor won't fix these issues by any means, they do make life living under such strange and stressful environments slightly easier. In other words, while jokes are not going to give the world a vaccine, they act as a "home remedy" of sorts to make life just a little bit better for the time being.

05

German Apples

___

Now that we've discovered how nations cope in the face of oppression using humor, our story does not end there. This chapter will begin our initial examination into how humor can be used to actively resist against threats facing the world.

The best example to show this is a relatively new threat: far-right nationalism. Far-right communities and white nationalism are quickly becoming international stains on the quest for justice and equality. The Southern Poverty Law Center has reported a dramatic increase in the number of white nationalist groups in the US for the fourth straight year.[43] The Anti-Defamation League reports a 182 percent increase in white supremacist incidents.[44] Perhaps most harrowing is that the number of terrorist attacks by far-right perpetrators has continued to increase far too quickly for anyone's liking.

White nationalism has given rise to counter-mobilization and counter-efforts against its spread. Anti-fascist

___

43 "Hate Groups Reach Record High," Southern Poverty Law Center, February 19, 2019.

44 "White Supremacists Step Up Off-Campus Propaganda Efforts in 2018," Anti-Defamation League, 2019.

activists use many tactics, but among its most prevalent is our subject: humor.

When Nazis mourned Rudolf Hass, a prominent member of the Nazi Party in Nazi Germany, with a march route, protesters turned it into an involuntary walkathon to raise money for anti-extremism social work. Without the Nazi sympathizers knowing, local individuals (and some businesses) "sponsored" the two hundred fifty or so participants of the march—for every meter they walked, 10 euros (~11.79 dollars) went to EXIT Deutschland, which helped people escape extremist groups. The Nazi sympathizers had no clue, that is, until on the march they saw that local residents had hung humorous signs everywhere, often with the slogan, "If only the Führer knew!" There was even a sign at the end of the march that thanked the marchers for their "donations."[45] The method was humor; the result was making the marchers look like absolute fools.

Others have played comical tuba music during Nazi marches or mailed pink women's underwear to violent Hindu conservatives who aim to "protect people from immorality" by assaulting those who partake in "immoral" activities. Humor in activism offers numerous benefits, such as cementing connections between members and enhancing mobilizing potential ("fun activism" typically has greater appeal than "nonviolent activism").

Humor as a tactic can easily be seen in 1960s West Germany. The Nazi authorities, even though there had been a process of de-Nazification, ended up in

45   David Layde, "German City Came Up With Genius Way Of Handling Neo-Nazis," Nova.ie, August 21, 2019.

important positions in business and politics. As such, when anti-communism activisms began to sprout on college campuses, the former Nazis in power could easily repress the students.

It was under this repression that activists aimed to find new forms of protest not confined by classic street demonstrations and clashes between the protestors and the police. Thus, the Spaßguerillas, or "fun-fighters," were born. A leading figure of one group of Spaßguerillas, the Sozialistischen Deutschen Studentenbund (SDS, 'German Socialist Student Union'), was Wolfgang Lefèvre, who wrote that "every event or demonstration should be inventively planned so that it is exciting and fun for students."[46] Playful tactics like throwing pies and pudding at the US Vice President Hubert Humphrey became commonplace—it was a way to show resistance against the United States in a way that made people want to join the group.

Fast forward to 2004, where the Front Deutscher Äpfel (literally 'Front of German Apples') was founded as a means of satirizing the far right after the far-right party won 9.2 percent of the overall vote.[47] The Front Deutscher Äpfel dressed in traditional fascist style: black button-downs with red armbands, but instead of a swastika, there was a silhouette of an apple. Within ten years, subgroups formed. The Front Deutscher Äpfel's founder, Alf Thum, was the 'Führer'; their Hitler Youth was the Nationales Frischobst Deutschland ('National Fresh Fruit of Germany'); and the Bund weicher Birnen ('League of

46   Michael C. Zeller, "How to Laugh Away the Far-Right: Lessons from Germany," openDemocracy, July 30, 2020.
47   2004 State Parliament Results, *Tagesschau*, 2004.

Soft Pears') was their League of German Girls. It was satire at its finest.

The Front Deutscher Äpfel had a platform as well, further mocking far-right nationalism: (1) no more foreign domination of German fruit stock, (2) expel tropical fruits, (3) get rid of the false representation of history propagated by the world conspiracy of grapefruits. To them, there needed to be a party based entirely on "fruit-based nationalism." By parodying the Nazi regime, they subverted the legitimacy of the rising far-right party in Germany.[48]

Even the police were helpless against the Front Deutscher Äpfel—they often laughed when the male leader of the Front Deutscher Äpfel shouted that he "wants to have the far-right leader's baby."[49] Their humor intentionally de-escalated the situation while also charming police officers deployed by the state.

There are few dreams that I would like to see come to light more than a manifestation of Front Deutscher Äpfel in other countries. Far-right nationalism (or any political party or group spewing hate) relies upon legitimacy, and as we know, humor allows for the subversion of such legitimacy. Front Deutscher Äpfel, along with other groups that we looked into in an earlier chapter, all use humor to ensure that far-right nationalist groups are unable to gain ground within a broader population. Combatting political thought through humor shouldn't just be limited to satirical parties, as Hungary's Two-Tailed

---

48   Front Deutscher Äpfel, "Nachrichten Aus Dem Führerhauptquartier," Front Deutscher Äpfel, November 1, 2018.

49   Florian Steglich, "Satire Gegen Rechtsradikale: Ein Apfel Für Die Nazis," Der Spiegel, Der Spiegel, May 2, 2006.

60 · TWO FISH IN A TANK
How Jokes Can Give Hope to Our Fractured World

Dog Party uses street art to parody the political elite.[50] There are multitudes of ways anyone can use comedy to combat political thought. Comedy allows for outsiders with keen insights to showcase their beliefs and garner traction, making it an invaluable skill in the digital age.

In reality, individual comedians can have a profound impact on the political arena. Some comedians have even run for office. While the obvious modern example is Ukrainian president Volodymyr Zelensky, a comedic actor who played the role of the President of Ukraine in the TV show *Servant of the People*, we can find an interesting case study in comedian Jón Gnarr, who ran for mayor of Reykjavik, Iceland's biggest city, in 2010.[51]

Gnarr created his own party, the Best Party, as a joke. Then, people realized that there were issues with the current political system and began to take him seriously. Gnarr's sincerity and honesty were rewarded with the mayor's seat. He would then enact very serious forms, such as the restructuring of banks and public-sector cutbacks during his four years in office. During debates, which are for all intents and purposes theatrical performances, comedians have several advantages. Not only do comedians make a more entertaining debate than politicians, they can create the viral moments on the fly through a clever witticism that reads the room perfectly. After all, comedians need to be able to read a room to garner success. In politics, this means that comedians can understand "the common person's" wants and needs far better than a politician could.

50   Soraya Sarhaddi Nelson, "Hungary's Satirical 'Two-Tailed Dog' Party Will Debut In Sunday Elections," NPR, April 7, 2018.

51   "Ukraine Election: Comedian Zelensky Wins Presidency by Landslide," *BBC News*, April 22, 2019.

Take TV comedian Jimmy Morales, who won the Guatemalan presidency with the simple slogan "Neither Corrupt Nor a Thief," which is apparently all his country wanted. Once again, we find that through subtle but intentional critique of the world through humor and satire, citizens gain hope for a better future and are willing to put their vote where they laugh.[52]

On November 25, 2014, the Front Deutscher Äpfel released eleven theses Martin-Luther-style, all about the need for satire in activism. Several of the theses are below, as they more eloquently describe the power of satire far better than I ever could:

(3) Satirical provocation in the name of emancipation does not shoot down. It shoots upward: At the social conditions and the character masks that they create.

(5) Is it the task of satire to formulate initiative proposals for a solution? NO! NO! NO! She is criticism. Critique of the existing is the end, satire the means.

(10) We call up to the balcony of the Hotel Abgrund (a predominantly upper-class school): "If you can't come down to the party, at least lean back and enjoy the show!"

(11) The satirists have only satirized the world in different ways, it is important to change it.[53]

Let's take those one by one and analyze them—and we will see that from them the importance of humor in response to threats like these are necessary:

---

52   Dominic Boyer, "Simply the Best: Parody and Political Sincerity in Iceland," *American Ethnologist* 40, no. 2 (2013): 276–87.

53   Front Deutscher Äpfel, "Thesen Über Satire Als Angewandten Punkrock," Front Deutscher Äpfel, January 31, 2015.

(3) Satirical provocation in the name of emancipation does not shoot down. It shoots upward: At the social conditions and the character masks that they create.

Critically, satire must be aimed upward at those in power or the structures of power that have segregated the oppressing from the oppressed. Poking fun at leaders is an important check on government power, especially in a democracy. Think of this like children on a playground. When the smaller kid mocks the bully, the bully totally has it coming and theoretically should be able to take the blows. Some people, myself included, would actually laud the smaller kid for sticking up to the bully. But when the bully mocks the smaller kid, no one is backing the bully.

When you have structural disadvantages against you, jokes made at your expense just aren't as funny. Molly Ivins, the former *New York Times* columnist, once said, "Satire is traditionally the weapon of the powerless against the powerful."

(5) Is it the task of satire to formulate initiative proposals for a solution? NO! NO! NO! She is criticism. Critique of the existing is the end, satire the means.

What satire does is unique—it points a finger at what is wrong. I would argue that this is just as, if not more, important than finding a solution. After all, what is a problem-solver to do when there are no problems that have been pointed out? Satire heightens the truth beyond the falsehoods—something that is getting repeatedly more difficult to do in the era of "fake news."

(11) The satirists have only satirized the world in different ways, it is important to change it.

As an example, John Oliver on his show, *Last Week Tonight*, always is attempting to start campaigns to right wrongs in the world. This comes from an inherent recognition that while satire is effective at making the truth heard, this means nothing when no one does anything about it. It would be similar to a politician going out into the streets, noticing trash on the ground, and proceeding to say "There's trash on the ground!" while walking away and not picking up the litter.

The more observant of you will notice that I skipped over the tenth thesis:

(10) We call up to the balcony of the Hotel Abgrund (a predominantly upper-class school): "If you can't come down to the party, at least lean back and enjoy the show!"

In response to satire, oppressors have three choices: join in, watch silently, or fight back. We can clearly see that Front Deutscher Äpfel is asking the upper-class to do one of the first two actions—but why not the third?

In reality, as we will discover in the next chapter, the worst thing that an oppressor can do is fight back against satire.

06

The Political Humor Paradox

———

In 1998, Otpor!, Serbia's nonviolent, pro-democracy movement, was just a tiny group of broke college students when they decided to play a prank. They took an oil barrel, taped a picture of the Serbian dictator Slobodan Milošević to it, and put it in the middle of Belgrade's largest shopping district. Next to it, Otpor! placed a baseball bat. Then, they grabbed a coffee and watched.

Before long, dozens of shoppers lined the streets of Belgrade for a chance to take a swing at "Milošević." Milošević was despised by many, but Serbians were too afraid to criticize for fear of imprisonment. Thirty minutes in, the police arrived—but what could they do?

They had no grounds to arrest the shoppers, and the police had no clue who the culprits were (remember that Otpor! was just relaxing in a nearby coffee shop, but the police didn't know that). So, what did they do? They arrested the barrel. The image of the two policemen quite literally dragging the barrel to their police car went viral for months on end. In the words of one member of Otpor!, "Milošević and his cronies became the laughing stock of the nation, and Otpor! became a household name." Otpor! called their version of nonviolent struggle against oppression as "laughtivism."[54]

In 2012, we saw a similar event in Siberia, where a "protest" brewed under Putin's Russia. I put "protest" in quotation marks because the Siberian pro-democracy protest featured no humans—only teddy bears, Lego characters, and *South Park* figurines, to name a few. The teddy bears each had signs that you would see at any other protest—"Putin is corrupt" and whatnot—but that was it. At this time, protests were met with staunch opposition by the government, where protesters would be arrested left and right; but when authorities arrived, they didn't see any culprits, because there were no humans there at all. So, what were they to do?

You guessed it, they arrested the toys. The toys were hauled off in official police cars to be detailed for their illegal behavior. Better yet, they imposed an official ban on all future toy protests. This ban went viral almost instantly, reminding dictators that laughter and humor are dangerous opposition forces.[55]

We are convinced that the only ways to combat oppression are with serious means. We protest, we debate, and we go to war. But because of what I call the political humor paradox, humor is an essential tool for combating oppression.

---

54   Srdja Popovic, "How We Used Laughter to Topple a Dictator," *Slate Magazine*, February 6, 2015.

55   Kevin O'Flynn, "Toys Cannot Hold Protest Because They Are Not Citizens of Russia, Officials Rule," *The Guardian*, February 15, 2012.

How Jokes Can Give Hope to Our Fractured World

The political humor paradox is relatively simple. In general, dictators and oppressors cannot do much to prevent political humor against them—there is simply no defense against it. If dictators try and fight back, they only appear more ridiculous, thus causing more political humor to manifest within the oppressed.

It is the goal of an oppressor to dehumanize their victims and give them no hope of change. Humor illustrates their victims' capabilities for free thought, and there is absolutely nothing that a dictator fears more. Put simply, the very existence of laughter and jokes means that a dictator has failed to dehumanize and demoralize their victims. This is humor with a definite purpose—that is, to ridicule the oppressors and keep the oppressed hopeful. It is a surprisingly reliable index of the morale of the oppressed; where there is humor, there is hope and resistance.

Moreover, the reactions to humor by the oppressors give an interesting insight into their own perceived strength. When oppressors can afford to ignore it, they believe they are strong; when oppressors react violently, they are not. And as multitudes of researchers before me have found, dictators are never confident in their success by their very nature. We know that an authoritarian ruler's repression creates fear, which then breeds uncertainty about how much support the ruler has; in response, the ruler is forced to repress further. In a similar manner, the political humor paradox tells us that if a ruler aims to be more repressive, the shutting down of humor only breeds more humor.

Moreover, as long as the oppressor knows that their victims ridicule them, they cannot be sure of their victory.

Oppressors thrive on knowing that the oppressed are afraid of them—humor dispels this very fear!

Surprisingly, perhaps the greatest example of the political humor paradox comes from 1930s Germany, where my Jewish ancestors were in concentration camps trying to survive to the next day. When I was younger, it seemed like every week I learned more and more about the atrocities of the Holocaust. Day after day, my ancestors never saw their families again, watched their friends disappear, and feared for their lives in ways we can only imagine. I kept wondering how we made it through.

And then I found the story of Antonin Obrdlik.

Antonin Obrdlik remembers what it was like living under Nazi occupation. He recalls the anger of the Germans in Czechoslovakia as they washed away inscriptions making fun of their führer, only for them to reappear again the next morning. To those under occupation, the Nazis' anger was hilarious.[56] The graffiti served as a no-cost, anonymous way of fighting back.

Two jokes, in particular, were extremely effective against the Nazi invaders of Czechoslovakia. The first involves a calendar and a pamphlet. Soon after war broke out, the German soldiers received and distributed a calendar of events that they believed would take place on future dates. According to the schedule, England was expected to "be on her knees no later than August 15, 1940." August 15 came and passed, and England was far from on her knees. Soon after, the Czechs distributed leaflets reading, "Do you know why Hitler has not invaded England yet?

56   Antonin J. Obrdlik, "'Gallows Humor'-A Sociological Phenomenon," *American Journal of Sociology* 47, no. 5 (March 1942): 709–16.

Because the German officers could not manage to learn in time all English irregular verbs." Another pamphlet distributed at roughly the same time read: "Do you know why the daylight-saving time has been exceptionally prolonged this year? Because Hitler promised that before the summer is over, he and his army will be in England." This pamphlet made the Germans furious—waves of mass arrests followed the spread of this pamphlet. Apparently, the Nazis did not enjoy being the butt of the jokes. And better yet, even the Nazis, people in control of a government that was at the time going to war with the world, couldn't fight back against it.

After these pamphlets were spread, it was near-impossible to find a Czech truly loyal to the Germans. According to one legend, one was found on an old man who proclaimed on the street that "Adolf Hitler is the greatest leader. The Germans are a noble nation. I would rather work for ten Germans than for one Czech." When the Germans asked what he did for a living, the Czech Nazi supporter reluctantly admitted to being a gravedigger.[57]

Often, waves of humor followed waves of restrictions or orders from Germany itself. When foreign broadcasts were declared a form of high treason, the following story allegedly occurred:

A Czech guest leaving the restaurant one evening says to his friend, "Good night. Now I am going to listen to the London and Paris broadcasts." He is overheard by a Nazi soldier and followed to his home. However, no radio can be found. "Do you listen to foreign broadcasts?" asks the German man suspiciously. The Czech replies, "Oh, yes, I

---

57   Ibid.

just can't help it." Then the Czech man kneels and puts his ear to the ground: "That's London there." After that, he puts his ear to the wall of the neighboring apartment and whispers: "That's Paris there." When the Nazi soldier hurries around to the adjacent flats, he finds that in one of them is a high official of the German SS administration, and in the other one, a German officer in uniform.[58]

In the example of the Jews during the Holocaust, jokes mocked the torture that the Nazis inflicted on them.

Take the example of survivor Lily Rickman. Upon arrival at the concentration camps, all prisoners were forced to shave their heads, further reducing them of their humanity. Lily Rickman laughed and called it a "free haircut." The laughter was rebellious, if not a little crazy. But it definitely caught the guards off-guard. Moreover, by saying that the Nazis gave her a free haircut, she made the Nazi guards think that they were doing her a favor.[59]

Moreover, if the Nazi guards joked about their prisoners, the Jews would laugh at the very same jokes. The ability to destabilize an oppressive situation by laughing at the expense of oneself was extraordinarily common for the Jews during the Holocaust. While the jokes were at one point a weapon used to oppress, Jews could use the same jokes to laugh at themselves—thus getting rid of any power the jokes may have.[60]

Holocaust survivor Elie Wiesel explored this concept in his novel *Gates of the Forest*. Gregor, the main character,

---

58   Ibid.

59   Whitney Carpenter, "Laughter in a Time of Tragedy: Examining Humor during the Holocaust," *Denison Journal of Religion* 9 (2010): 12–25.

60   Chaya Ostrower, "Humor as a Defense Mechanism during the Holocaust," *Interpretation: A Journal of Bible and Theology* 69, no. 2 (March 23, 2015): 183–95.

is orphaned by the Holocaust. Gregor is hiding in a cave when he meets Gavriel, who teaches Gregor how to employ laughter to catch his oppressors off-guard. Gavriel's humor allowed him to rise above anti-Semitism because of his laughter.[61] To laugh in the face of fear allows that fear to dissipate. Laughter becomes a concealed dagger for Gavriel against his oppressors.

One Holocaust survivor remembered how "one day [the Nazi guards] were hitting us black and blue, and then they were laughing while we made fun of them."[62] The guards ended up laughing as well—thus stopping the assault. The Nazis may have gotten the last shot, but the Jews got the last laugh.

The political humor paradox gives us insight into the power of humor as a resistance tool. We have seen how comedy has been used in the face of totalitarianism and in spite of oppression. The lesson is clear: we must use comedy as a tool of resistance. It is not to be used all the time, but when we want to seriously combat oppression, we must joke about it. This concept is counterintuitive, but history tells us that those who made fun of their oppressors had one of two things happen. First, the oppressor ignored it, thus elevating the spirits of the oppressed through laughter, or second, the oppressor tried to stifle the laughter in some ridiculous way which in turn spawned more jokes. This is the beauty of the political humor paradox: it works. Sometimes we must laugh in the face of oppression. By making the oppressor the butt of the joke, the oppressed gain power over

---

61   Elie Wiesel, *The Gates of the Forest*. (New York, New York: Schocken Books, 1996).

62   Carpenter, "Laughter," *Denison Journal*.

issues and people that challenge them. It challenges and changes the power structures—even just a slight bit.

Ultimately, we have seen throughout the course of this chapter how comedy can be used as an act of resistance toward the government. Take Otpor!, who infamously placed a bat next to a barrel with their authoritarian leader's picture on it—this, I believe, should be done more often and in other locales to fight against freedom of speech restrictions. We also have examples such as the Siberian Toy Protest where comedy was easily used in the face of totalitarianism.

My suggestion follows a similar train of thought: we must embrace comedy as a form of resistance. In my dream world, this would take place through a comedy festival held outside of whatever political body is causing trouble. For example, in the US, I envision a comedy festival on the White House lawn (or, at the very least, the National Mall) where people talk comedically about racial issues in the United States. On another level, when protesting war or other international crises, a comedy festival could bring to light significant issues that may not be within the national conscience. Imagine television and radio crews all covering the event as it occurred in real time, and because people would laugh while watching the event, people would be more likely to turn into and pay attention to this event as opposed to a protest march.

We see examples of this manifesting itself today, the most prominent example of which are the dozens of comedians, such as Dave Chappelle or Chris Rock, who have used humor to critique the systemic oppression painfully apparent within the United States.[63, 64] As the current *SNL* writer Jasmine Pierce said in a recent interview with Vulture, "This is the first time we're getting to expose the absurdities of our daily life and everyone is listening. Being Black in a white world is the joke; we just have to write it down."[65] The US government can do nothing to stop them from doing so—any action that the government takes to prevent comedians from joking will only be met with more humor from some of the funniest people alive right now.

But concerning international crises, we have precedent in Mark Thomas, a comedian who in 2004 encouraged his audience to participate in protests against the Iraq War through humorous, but effective, means. He suggested the day of a protest march:

If you were on the demonstration today—[or if] you go tomorrow—the cops will go filming ya, right? If you were on that demonstration in London—the big f***ing Ministry of Defense people will have filmed every single f***ing demonstrator. Under the Data Protection Act, you are entitled to claim your video image. Write in. Write in: "Dear Police Officer—Dear M.O.D. [Ministry of Defense]. I was on the march. I do believe you were filming. Under the Data Protection Act, I would like to declare all the video images of me. Here is a passport photograph, a copy of a recent utility bill—ah, proof of where I live—and a check for ten pounds which you're obliged to, er, to ask for but you don't necessarily have to cash in. I would like all video images of me. I do note that any video images of other

---

63   *8:46*, YouTube, 2020.

64   *Tamborine*, Netflix, 2018.

65   Taylor Garron, "What's So Funny About Being Black?" *Vulture*, June 19, 2020.

people included on the tape would be illegal and in breach of the Data Protection Act." [Laugh]. "Find me if you can."

He then goes on to imagine a police officer sat in a room watching endless reams of footage, then builds to a big laugh and applause as he says: "And if we all f***ing did it, it'd be f***ing great! In fact, even if you're not on the march, f***ing do it—that's even more important! Every one of you, join in!" Thomas makes direct action more accessible; for those watching the comedy protest at home, they are able to do something as simple as write a letter to show support. In doing so, he demystifies the state's narrative about the war and provides his own. Thomas argues that the war is just a strategic maneuver designed to defend the American empire. Thomas summarizes with the final lines of his show: "And I'll tell you what it's about, for each and every one of us. It's about when we wake up in the morning, and we look at ourselves in the bathroom mirror, can we live with what we see? Good luck and thanks for coming."[66]

Imagine what could happen with an audience larger than a theater; larger than those who can hear him at a protest. When at a festival broadcasted on television (and, I assume, posted on video-sharing websites like YouTube and on social media platforms), the message will spread over the entire world, since the world will be watching. People who joke and laugh about serious problems are more likely to act toward solving those problems, thus making resistance movements more likely.

And if the authorities try and shut it down? Remember the political humor paradox—their attempts to shut

66   Sophie Quirk, "Preaching to the Converted? How Political Comedy Matters," *Humor* 29, no. 2 (April 29, 2016): 243–60.

down the comedy festival would only result in absolute hilarity.

I am aware that this is one of my more outlandish, but potentially effective, ideas. So, if we take ourselves back down into reality, we will see that the lesson is clear: we must use comedy as a tool of resistance. It is not to be used all the time, but when we want to spread awareness of an issue (especially an international one), we must joke about it. This concept is counterintuitive, but history tells us that those who made fun of their oppressors had one of two things happen: the oppressor ignored it, thus elevating the spirits of the oppressed through laughter, or the oppressor tried to stifle the laughter through some manner, which in turn caused the political humor paradox to take place. Sometimes we must laugh in the face of oppression. By making the oppressor the butt of the joke, the oppressed gain power over issues that challenge them.

I shall leave you with the story of my sister, who was the subject of an anti-Semitic attack when she was called a "rich Jew" at elementary school. She promptly pulled out a ten-dollar bill, gave it to her bully, and said, "Buy some better insults."

07

Jon, Hasan, and John

———

I remember vividly the first time I ever saw Jon Stewart grace my television screen. It was 2008, where then-Senator Barack Obama and Senator John McCain were both vying to be the next most powerful man in the world: the United States' President. I laughed at Stewart's hilarious jokes, quips, and over-the-top animations and special effects.

But for those just a generation older than me, the 2008 financial crisis was ongoing and terrifying. In the midst of the most severe global recession since the Great Depression, the United States was battered and bruised. The country seemingly had never been more divided between the rich and the poor—and we had never been more hopeless.

Enter Jon Stewart, the man who once described himself in high school as "very into Eugene Debs and a bit of a leftist."[67] Stewart was given somewhat of an impossible task when he first started on *The Daily Show* in 1999: make people laugh while giving them the news.

———
67   Alison Adato, "Anchor Astray," Earthlink.net, May 2000.

It had been done before. In 1966, *The Frost Report* was created on UK airwaves, where the host David Frost would use sketch comedy to critique the politicians for the day.[68] Stewart, unlike his predecessor Craig Kilborn, followed the idea of critiquing politicians—but instead of using sketch comedy as a medium, Stewart chose to parody a news desk. While under Kilborn the focus of the show was on human interest stories, Stewart wished to steer the show directly into the political arena. Stewart's style was marked by a playful nature, which allowed him to talk about complex news topics that typically seemed unapproachable to the average person.

As Christy Wallover, the exhibit writer for the Newseum in Washington, DC, once said, "He put news and politics and cultural significance in a way that was approachable."[69]

Take for example the humanitarian crisis in Gaza. A complicated crisis half the world away from the United States, it can appear to some (particularly those in the midwestern areas where I grew up) that the conflict is hopeless. In the words of someone I once got to talking to at a Starbucks, "That thing over there is hopeless—and I ain't even gonna begin to understand it because it's hopeless for me to do so."

But then Jon Stewart enters the conversation. When he interviewed the former Secretary of State Hillary Clinton on the humanitarian crisis in 2014, he asked if those living in Gaza could view Hamas as "freedom fighters." It was a sobering and serious question that one would not

68   Sarah J. Burton, "More than Entertainment: The Role of Satirical News in Dissent, Deliberation and Democracy," Thesis, The Pennsylvania State University Graduate School College of Communications, 2010.

69   Evan Haynos, "The Newseum's New 'Daily Show' Exhibit Reminds Us of Jon Stewart's Impact," The Diamondback, August 27, 2020.

expect from a show on Comedy Central, but it worked. Because nearly every question leading up to this conversation was humorous in nature, both Stewart and Clinton appeared friendly, as if they were cool college professors that one could go visit during office hours.[70]

They seemed approachable, and thus, the issue seemed approachable. The hopelessness that Americans felt at such an issue suddenly appeared as a complex, yet understandable topic—one that the American public would later question Clinton about during her 2016 presidential campaign.

What political comedians like Stewart are able to do is offer an 'inside' approach to what appears to be a very confusing and difficult world. They aren't political reporters, nor are they pure comedians—they walk a thin line that gives them authority without the authoritativeness.

This philosophy of making complex issues approachable, thus giving the hope to people that they could change major international injustices, is clear when one takes a look at Jon Stewart's news team. Many of those on his rotating group of correspondents, who were dubbed "The Best F#@ing News Team," went on to host similar shows of their own. Most notably for our purposes, let's take a look at two correspondents: Hasan Minhaj and John Oliver.

In March 2019, comedian Hasan Minhaj, on his Netflix show *Patriot Act*, took aim at another issue halfway around the world: the Indian Prime Minister, Narendra Modi.

Extremely few outside of India not directly connected to the country understood what was going on—which

70   Maggie Haberman, "Clinton Talks Gaza, Media Scrutiny," *POLITICO*, July 16, 2014

is why *Patriot Act* is so powerful. In just over a half hour, Minhaj is able to show his viewers the atrocities going on in the world and what each individual can do to solve them.[71] Critically, the sad news is repeatedly interrupted by jokes—making the experience of watching *Patriot Act* both informational and interesting.

Patriot Act's episode made waves, both on social media and within government circles. On social media, commentators lauded him. One tweet read, "Farmer issues got more coverage in Hasan Minhaj's *Patriot Act* episode than they have received in the last many months on Indian television."[72] Another tweet from Vishal Dadlani, an Indian singer and composer, read, "You HAVE to watch this show (and especially this episode if you live/vote in India)."[73]

The Indian government wasn't as keen about the episode, as shown by Minhaj trying to gain entry to the 'Howdy Modi' event with Indian Prime Minister Modi and US President Donald Trump on September 22, 2019. As Minhaj would later explain on *Late Night with Seth Meyers*,

"We submit our press credentials, immediately get an e-mail back through saying, 'We're out of space.' I was like 'word'...like I've been to Indian weddings, you just walk in. You're out of space in a football stadium? Nah."

So, I recheck with the organizers, 'Hey guys it's my community, you get it?' I want to be there. And they're like, 'We're out of space but we'll discuss it.' I'm like 'okay' and

---

71   "Indian Elections," Episode, *Patriot Act with Hasan Minhaj* 2, no. 6. Netflix, March 17, 2019.

72   Aakriti, Twitter Post, March 17, 2019, 7:48 a.m.

73   Vishal Dadlani, Twitter Post, March 19, 2019, 12:51 a.m.

How Jokes Can Give Hope to Our Fractured World

said, 'I'm sorry for making fun of cricket. It's not a sport for farms, it's an international game that's taking over the world.' They replied, 'No, some of the comments you made about Prime Minister Modi were not appreciated and you've been blacklisted.'

Instead, Minhaj watched the dual speech on his phone in the parking lot. In the speech itself, many Indian-Americans were being honored for their contributions to the arts, including Minhaj himself. Minhaj quipped, "They were honoring me for my comedy while also blackmailing and blackballing me and kicking me out for my comedy. It is the most Indian thing ever. They were like, 'We're proud of you but we'll never say it to your face."[74]

But what Minhaj's show did was bring hope to many in the Indian-American community that the issues they saw within India were solvable. It gave them hope that although the Indian government may have its problems, they can be solved. As one Indian father wrote on twitter, "Both my daughters will be voting for the first time in 2019. They asked me who to vote for? I told them—Watch [the episode]."[75]

This wasn't the first time Minhaj had gotten into international trouble. In October 2018, *Patriot Act* ran a segment on Saudi Arabia, specifically about the Crown Prince of Saudi Arabia, Mohammed bin Salman. This episode challenged popular views that the Crown Prince was revolutionary—while women could now drive in Saudi

---

74   Late Night with Seth Meyers, "Hasan Minhaj Was Barred from an Indian Political Rally That Trump Attended," YouTube video, 6:41, September 24, 2019.

75   "Hasan Minhaj Show: Hasan Minhaj Decided to Talk Indian Politics, and Twitter Can't Keep Calm," *The Economic Times*, March 19, 2019.

Arabia, the Crown Prince also authorized the killing of journalist Jamal Khashoggi. Domestically, Minhaj pointed out how an online manual used for US troops deployed to Saudi Arabia described the local population as a "mixture of Negro blood from slaves imported from Africa." (Minhaj's next line: "Oh America, even in boring, technical manuals, you still somehow manage to be racist.")[76] Within a month of the episode's release, the US military issued an apology and removed the manual.[77]

Internationally, Minhaj's self-proclaimed "woke Ted Talk" had been removed from Netflix's Saudi Arabia service. This removal was after Saudi Arabia's Communications and Information Technology Commission issued a request to Netflix to take it down over concerns regarding content.[78] Minhaj quipped in response, "A request? Does MBS think Netflix is a wedding DJ? 'Yeah, quick request. You wanna take down just that one episode that's criticizing me and then just play Usher's "Yeah"?' A request is when a neighbor tells you to turn the music down. A demand is when that neighbor is [professional mixed martial artist and boxer] Conor McGregor and you're in his parking spot."[79]

Minhaj would later note that the eighteen-minute critique of the Crown Prince was still up on YouTube ("Clearly, the

76   "Saudi Arabia," Episode, *Patriot Act with Hasan Minhaj* 1, no. 2. Netflix, October 28, 2018.

77   Thomas Gibbons-Neff, "American Military Apologizes for Booklet With Racially Offensive Language," *The New York Times*, November 1, 2018.

78   Ahmed Al Omran, "Netflix Pulls Episode of Comedy Show in Saudi Arabia," *Financial Times*, January 1, 2019.

79   "Content Moderation and Free Speech," Episode. *Patriot Act with Hasan Minhaj* 1, no. 7. Netflix, December 2, 2018.

How Jokes Can Give Hope to Our Fractured World

best way to stop people from watching something is to ban it, make it trend online, and then leave it up on YouTube").[80]

Once again, we see the power of comedy: why would a foreign government take down what essentially mounts to a thirty-minute standup set?

Saudi Arabia stated that under article six of their anti-cybercrime law, any content that touches on religious values, public order, or public morals is prohibited—however, shows such as *BoJack Horseman* (which prominently features drugs and alcohol) and *The Chilling Adventures of Sabrina*, which, as Minhaj notes, "features literal devil worship and a lot of premarital witch sex," remain up.[81]

The only episode taken off the air was that single episode of *Patriot Act*—the one that called for critique and change to the Saudi regime. No episodes of *BoJack Horseman* were taken off, but to be fair, *BoJack Horseman* never critiqued a sitting regime. From this, we can know that this censorship is less about "religious values, public order, or public morals" and more about Minhaj blatantly telling the world that change is possible—and perhaps more importantly, that there is hope for change in a regime that has acted horrifically.

John Oliver takes a similar approach in his show *Last Week Tonight with John Oliver*. There is rarely a topic of global significance that John Oliver hasn't talked about on his weekly half-hour show, *Last Week Tonight*.

To illustrate this fact, I used a random number generator and randomly selected seven episodes out of the two hundred episodes just to see the results. Here's what I got from my hardly-scientific experiment:

---

80   Hasan Minhaj, Twitter Post, January 2, 2019, 2:04 p.m.

81   "Content Moderation," *Patriot Act*, 2018.

6. FIFA.

93. Tibetan sovereignty debate and human rights in Tibet.

17. Scottish independence referendum.

182. COVID-19 pandemic and governmental response in the US.

97. Gerrymandering in the United States.

110. 2017 North Korea crisis.

29. Voting rights in the US territories.

These topics scratch the surface of the wide breadth of Oliver's show. Let's take two of them and explore the impact that John Oliver's segments had on the topics (hint: it was significant).

6. FIFA. In 2014, Oliver highlighted corruption at the world's largest and most powerful sports organization. As *Time Magazine* explains, "Oliver covers it all from sexist remarks by the organization's top official to poor treatment of migrant workers constructing World Cup stadiums." Oliver brought key awareness to the situation unfolding—with many arrests following the airing of his show by US officials. One year later, Oliver brought another scathing takedown of the organization, calling for FIFA president Sepp Blatter to step down. "The problem is all the arrests in the world are going to change nothing as long as Blatter is still there," Oliver said. "To truly kill a snake, you must cut off its head—or, in this case, its asshole."[82] Less than forty-eight hours later, Blatter abruptly announced his resignation as President.[83]

82 "FIFA and the World Cup," Episode, *Last Week Tonight with John Oliver* 1, no. 6. HBO, June 8, 2014.

83 Justin Worland, "FIFA Corruption Arrests: What John Oliver Said About the Soccer Group," *Time*, May 27, 2015.

29. Voting Rights in the US territories. On March 8, 2015, Oliver highlighted the four million people living in US island territories (including the Virgin Islands, Guam, and Puerto Rico). Oliver drew awareness to their lack of the right to vote due to the "Insular Cases" of the early twentieth century, which restrict some constitutional rights to residents of US territories. Highlighting the lack of medical care and the contradictory treatment of veterans on these islands, the world learned the unjust treatment of these citizens.[84] In the court of appeals for the Ninth Circuit in the US, a judge had to have caught the episode, as the episode was cited within her official opinion.[85]

Now, I'm going to be a little more focused on which topics I cover, since this is a book about international relations. A segment on the then Prime Minister of Australia, Tony Abbott, received the headline of "Tony Abbott roasted by John Oliver on HBO show *Last Week Tonight*" in the *Sydney Morning Herald* the following day after the clip went viral on Australian Twitter.[86]

After a segment on the military government of Thailand, within which Oliver called Crown Prince Vajiralongkorn a "buffoon" and an "idiot," Oliver was listed as "undermining the royal institution." In a document seen by VICE, Thailand's military junta called the National Council of Peace and Order expressed concerns and paranoia about Oliver's activities. This document was written four days

84   "Voting Rights for US Territories," Episode, *Last Week Tonight with John Oliver* 2, no. 5. HBO, March 8, 2015.

85   Paeste, Paeste, Zapanta and Zapanta v. Guam, Calvo, Mangloña and Camacho (United States Court of Appeals for the Ninth Circut August 26, 2015).

86   Nick Toscano, "Tony Abbott Roasted by John Oliver on HBO Show Last Week Tonight," *The Sydney Morning Herald*, June 2, 2014.

after the show aired. Oliver gained this title after showing a clip of leaked footage of a birthday party beside a swimming pool which featured the crown prince and his topless wife. The royal couple is shown blowing out candles with their pet poodle Foo Foo (who also holds the rank of air chief marshal in the Royal Thai Air Force). Oliver quipped after hearing of the news, "You're telling me they're not supposed to make fun of that? That's entrapment!"[87]

During a June 2018 episode, Oliver discussed Xi Jinping, the General Secretary of the Communist Party of China, specifically criticizing his dictatorship tendencies and Jinping's excessive censorship of Chinese media. Immediately following the episode, the phrases "John Oliver" and "*Last Week Tonight*" were blocked from Sina Weibo, a Chinese social media platform.[88]

The real-world change and action that has been taken on issues highlighted by Oliver's show have been given a name: "the John Oliver Effect." The phenomenon works by spreading awareness of a particular issue, which then inspires Oliver's viewers to take action on the issues Oliver highlights.[89] While only a few viewers actually take action, when Oliver's average viewership is about one million per episode (not including over 2.5 billion total views on YouTube, a Facebook page with over 2.6 million likes, and a Twitter account with over three million followers), even a small number of individuals who are made aware of these injustices taking actions is more than enough to influence all levels of government—from local government to international organizations.

87   Andrew MacGregor Marshall, "Thailand's Military Government Thinks John Oliver Is a Threat to Its Monarchy," *VICE*, July 24, 2014.

88   "Why You Can't Talk about John Oliver in China," *BBC News*, June 21, 2018.

89   Victor Luckerson, "The John Oliver Effect: The HBO Host's Real-World Impact," *Time*, July 10, 2015.

For what it's worth, Oliver has openly ridiculed the idea on his show, calling the term "completely meaningless."[90]

But why does John Oliver spark so much controversy? And why is there even consideration of a "John Oliver Effect"?

I find that his newest headline offers some insight, which was plastered on a Times Square screen right above a Walgreens: "If there's hope for him, there's hope for all of us."[91]

In making complex and lofty issues approachable through comedy, individuals (both victims of such issues and those who aren't even aware of them) are able to understand the issues and act on them, because viewers genuinely believe that their actions can make a difference—a concept necessary to explore. In fact, we'll do that in the very next chapter.

---

90   "Money," Episode, *Last Week Tonight with John Oliver* 3, no. 15. HBO, June 12, 2016.

91   Ed Mazza, "John Oliver's Hilariously Awkward Throwback Photo Will Give You Hope," *HuffPost*, February 10, 2020.

08

Wagging the Dog

Esteban Gast, a lifelong comedian, remembers reading all about *Will and Grace*—the comedy series about a woman and her gay best friend that ran on NBC from 1998 to 2006. "I remember reading that *Will and Grace* has done more for gay rights than anything else because we fear what we don't know. [The show] makes you laugh in this beautiful way—it makes you no longer scared." Then-Vice President Joe Biden has expressed a similar statement before, theorizing that "*Will and Grace* probably did more to educate the American public than almost anything anybody's ever done so far."[92]

But why? Why would a sitcom make these waves in the social policy sphere? For Gast, the answer is simple: "When you're laughing, you're open to new ideas."

Gast understands this concept of humanization intimately. When he came to the continental United States from Puerto Rico, Gast was an outsider. He was American, but others didn't see him as such. When he began to learn English, he had a heavy accent. This difference

---

92   Caitlin McDevitt, "'Will & Grace' Applaud Joe Biden," *POLITICO*, May 7, 2012.

made him an instant outsider around his classmates, and as such, they bullied him. "It was easy not to see me as human. People would do whatever the heck they wanted since I couldn't communicate with them."

He knew that he had two options: he could either fight someone or play mental and emotional warfare through comedy. Gast couldn't resist his bullies physically, but what he did have was an incredible sense of wit. He realized that making fun of them with words served a dual purpose: first, and perhaps most importantly for a young child being bullied, words hurt more and cut deeper, especially coming from someone whose first language wasn't English. Second, being silly triggered a sense of empathy—it's impossible to punch someone who is making silly faces or laughing. For Gast, humor humanized himself in a culture he barely knew and wasn't keen on accepting him in the first place.

Gast, who is now a comedian (or as he puts it, a "professional storyteller"), uses comedy to tell the rigors of the immigration system. "It has its ups and downs, but also it's bureaucratic and ten times worse than [the NBC Sitcom] *The Office*. [The immigration system] has got this ridiculousness." But Gast isn't concerned with preaching to the choir—he knows that there are people out there who agree with him. Instead, Gast prefers to talk to people who actively come see his show—the same people who he aims to connect with, and possibly convince, through his humorous stories.

Gast maintains that he has convinced people to change their minds about immigration policies through his stories—which begs the question: can comedians like Gast, or comedy news shows like we discussed last chapter, or any other comedy, actually change anything?

What we have seen is a rise in comedy-focused information. Topics are often serious, but their methods used to transmit information about those topics often are not serious. Moreover, comedy sources of information such as these are designed to both elicit pleasure while also calling for judgment—it is unusual for viewers of CNN to crack a smile; for viewers of satirical news shows, it is unusual not to.

This leads us down the road to presenting arguments through comical means. It is entertainment with a purpose; the goal is to convince but in as non-hostile a way as possible. We intuitively know that topics treated in a humorous way are often perceived as less offensive than when presented seriously. If a show can present information or argument without eliciting a negative audience reaction (as CNN and Fox News are prone to do), then employing it could be a promising way to incite attitude change. Research consistently indicates that humor reduces counter-argumentation, or argument scrutiny, in response to the premise of that humorous text.[93]

For many individuals who are not as interested in politics or foreign policy, comedic news is an alternative to the hard news media as a world of information. This phenomenon, I argue, is an extremely good thing. As UCLA researcher Matthew Baum notes, "If a substantial portion of the public that would otherwise remain aloof from politics is able to learn about high-profile political

---

93 Dannagal Goldthwaite Young, "The Privileged Role of the Late-Night Joke: Exploring Humor's Role in Disrupting Argument Scrutiny," *Media Psychology* 11, no. 1 (March 19, 2008): 119–42.

issues, such as foreign crises, from the soft news media, this may expand the size of the attentive public, at least in times of crisis...a great deal of research has shown that intense public scrutiny, when it arises, can influence policymakers, both in Congress and the White House."[94]

Baum's study begins with an interesting discovery—that *Entertainment Tonight* and *The Oprah Winfrey Show* are watched by about the same number of households as the evening newscasts of the major TV networks. Moreover, soft news programs have covered every major US foreign military crisis since 1990, including the Persian Gulf War, the crises with Iraq, and US foreign crisis with Somalia, Haiti, Bosnia, and Kosovo. The coverage isn't sparse by any means—one tabloid news program, *Extra*, mentioned the foreign crises in over half the total number of *World News Tonight* shows. Predictably, there was less coverage (as network newscasts frequently present multiple stories on a given topic within a single broadcast with greater coverage), but this is a far from trivial observation.

Critically, comedic news and so-called "hard news" cover foreign policy news in drastically different manners. While hard news outlets typically cover political stories in unappealing and complex manners, comedy news purposely frame issues in accessible terms by emphasizing the dramatic and sensational human-interest stories—exactly the type of stories that would be of interest to an audience focused on entertainment as opposed to information. This emphasis on entertainment, once again, is a

---

94   Matthew A. Baum, "Sex, Lies, and War: How Soft News Brings Foreign Policy to the Inattentive Public," *American Political Science Review* 96, no. 1 (March 2002): 91–109.

good thing; by making news about foreign issues accessible, comedy news programs increase the likelihood that viewers uninterested in foreign policy will pay attention to and learn about these crises.

Baum notes a particularly interesting example in Bosnia:

[I]n mid-1995, in covering the escalating US military involvement in Bosnia, a review of the nightly news broadcasts of the three major networks indicates that they addressed a broad range of issues—including international diplomacy, military tactics, the role of NATO, 'nation building,' and ethnic cleansing, to name only a few. In contrast, the soft news media devoted most of their coverage to a single dramatic story: the travails of US fighter pilot Scott O'Grady, who was shot down over enemy territory on June 2, 1995. Captain O'Grady's heroic story of surviving behind enemy lines for five days on a diet of insects and grass, before being rescued by NATO forces, represented an ideal...human drama.[95]

Of the thirty-five total broadcasts on soft/comedy news sources about Bosnia, thirty of them (86 percent) featured the O'Grady story. Juxtapose this percentage to traditional hard news sources, who also covered the story. The difference is that the O'Grady story is one of many stories about military involvement in Bosnia. The story was only covered in thirteen of fifty-seven (23 percent) national news broadcasts about Bosnia.

Three years later, President Bill Clinton testified in front of a grand jury regarding his relationship with intern Monica Lewinsky. Three days after that, the US launched cruise missile strikes against suspected terrorist targets

---

95   Ibid.

in Sudan and Afghanistan. Once again, traditional news outlets and comedy outlets both covered the event—albeit in different ways. Hard news coverage covered everything from circumstances "on the ground," analyzing military tactics, profiling Osama bin Laden, and so on. Comedic sources focused on the uncanny parallels between real-world events and the slightly obscure movie, *Wag the Dog*. In *Wag the Dog*, a fictional president hires a Hollywood producer to "produce" a falsified war to distract the public from his involvement in a sex scandal.

This eerily similar situation was dramatic—in the week following the attacks, thirty-five of forty-six (76 percent) comedy news stories featured the *Wag the Dog* similarity, continuously raising the question as to whether or not the President launched the missile strikes to distract the nation from the Lewinsky scandal (a situation commonly referred to as the diversionary hypothesis). In contrast, hard news sources only mentioned either *Wag the Dog* or the Lewinsky scandal in eleven of sixty-nine (16 percent) of stories on the missile strikes.[96]

This begs the question, why do these shows matter? And why is comedy necessary?

When I had the chance to interview one of the head writers of *Patriot Act*, Seth Weitberg, he explained the process of creating a political comedy show. First, as a large team of Peabody-award-winning investigative journalists assist in the production of the show, they craft an argument and a story around a particular topic of interest to them. Comedy had no role here; in the words

---

96   Ibid.

of Weitberg, "When we were looking for stories and topics, comedy was rarely part of the consideration. It was almost always, what's the journalistic thing we want to explore and dive into? What's the systemic issue we want to bring light to or learn more about?" The jokes come after the story has been crafted and after the argument has been made. The joke writing comes in at the very end to add some lightness and fun to those stories. It is, essentially, a twenty-minute, heavily researched argumentative essay where jokes are peppered in. "There's sort of a candy-coated shell around all the hard truths."

So why add comedy to the mix? The answer is relatively simple: comedy makes heavy topics palatable. As Weitberg quipped, "People want information, they want to know stuff. But sitting down and reading a ten-thousand-word ProPublica article is not always easy work. The beauty of television comedy is that the writers and comedians are able to synthesize and package stuff with the comedy in a way that is much more digestible."

But does this mean anything? With more and more individuals choosing humorous programming as opposed to serious programming, we must ask if there are any meaningful implications.

What comedy news sources do is, as Baum describes, "piggyback" important information through entertainment-oriented information. This "piggybacking" allows individuals to learn about politics passively, even if they aren't interested in nor motivated to learn about the topics at hand. As a result, the information becomes an incidental byproduct of paying attention to entertainment-oriented information. For instance, individuals unwilling to read about foreign policy issues in the newspaper may be willing to watch the same issue play out live before their eyes like a soap opera. By "piggybacking," individuals who don't normally seek political information still receive some information about foreign policy, even if the intrinsic interests in the subjects are low.

This phenomenon is not only logical, but backed by statistical research as well. As expected, consumption of hard news and interests in international affairs is strongly associated with attentiveness to foreign crises. Where it gets interesting is Baum's next discovery: that exposure to soft/comedic news is positively and significantly associated with knowledge about foreign crises. Even individuals who follow international affairs loosely appear to learn about the issues through soft or comedy news sources. Baum notes that among the respondents who follow international affairs "not at all closely," as attentiveness to news media increases from its lowest to its highest levels, the probability of following the Israel-Lebanon conflict more than "not at all closely" increases by 38 percentage points (from 0.40 to 0.78). The corresponding increases for the congressional antiterrorism debate and Bosnia are 58 percentage points (from 0.34 to 0.92) and 47 percentage points (from 0.46 to 0.93) respectively.

This conclusion supports the theory that respondents uninterested in international affairs are nonetheless exposed to relevant information about foreign policy issues through the elastic news media sources. The impact of elastic news is wide-ranging: when Baum asked about the Northern Ireland conflict and peace process, as exposure to elastic news sources increases from its minimum to its maximum values, the probability

How Jokes Can Give Hope to Our Fractured World

of having an opinion about the crisis and peace deal (a typical indicator of attentiveness to the issue) increased by up to 25 percentage points. The probability of having an opinion increased by 55 percentage points for those without a college degree. This result makes it clear: elastic news sources impact citizens' views on foreign policy, which in turn influences the foreign policy itself.

This phenomenon is unique to foreign policy crises—when Baum reran a similar test with the 1996 US presidential primaries, there was no similar nor significant effect.

Baum's statistical investigations demonstrate that individuals learn about foreign policy issues (such as war) but not less dramatic issues (such as presidential primaries) from soft and comedic news without any intention to learn when they turned on the television.

Understanding that public opinion can influence policy outcomes, particularly in foreign policy areas, soft and comedic news media coverage of foreign policy can and does have significant practical consequences for the international system. Additionally, while many watchers of soft or comedic news programs are not the most politically active outside of elections, they do vote in significant numbers.[97]

This can actually help save a democracy, surprisingly, for two reasons. First, comedic news outlets allow for political and military leaders to communicate with large segments of the population that have traditionally tuned out foreign affairs in their entirety. (Yes, Jimmy Fallon

---

97   Dannagal G. Young, "Theories and Effects of Political Humor: Discounting Cues, Gateways, and the Impact of Incongruities," *The Oxford Handbook of Political Communication*, 2014.

and Stephen Colbert may actually be saving our democracy by inviting presidents onto their respective shows.) Jimmy Fallon's recurring segment, "Slow Jam the News," which has featured presidents and political candidates, allows for news to be shared in a funny way that invites those tuning in for comedy to learn about political issues and the politicians themselves—Washington, DC seems approachable and normal as opposed to a far-off land of men and women in suits.

As an added bonus, this can help politicians expand their support coalitions beyond traditionally politically-focused members of the voting population. Broader coalitions, in turn, can translate into more trust in government, leading to more effective leadership in troubling times (such as war).

Second, the introduction of comedy into news sources lead to a more broadly attentive population, which would yield more participation in the political process (e.g. voting, protesting, voicing concerns publicly). I, alongside many, consider this a desirable outcome.

PART III

09

How to Topple
North Korea

When I originally started to write this book, I became convinced that humor could be a weapon in war. I figured that if the United States were to make fun of Russia or China, then Russia or China would look foolish in return and would thus lose their legitimacy in the international system. This made inherent sense to me—why couldn't the political humor paradox translate over into inter-state competition?

The answer is relatively simple: there is an expectation of formality between states, especially within war or any kind of conflict. To joke about a given conflict is seen as taboo. After all, joking about death, especially when leaders chose to go into a given conflict, is somewhat inhumane and inconsiderate.

Moreover, when states are at war, especially a long-winded and relatively equal war (think either of the World Wars), there is no side that is drastically more powerful than the other—instead of one side "punching up" against their adversaries, it's more like a jab right in front of them. As such, both sides have the ability to joke effectively, thus negating any benefits that the political humor paradox may have.

But this represented a fault in my conception of conflict: when we think of war we think of Country A's military or government in conflict with Country B's military or government. But then I realized that there is an entire other aspect of war too often forgotten about: Country A's relationship with Country B's citizenry.

The people. We've spent the entirety of this book so far going over how people use humor against governments, but what about when governments use humor and satire as a vehicle for citizens of another country to critique their own government? Is it possible for a government to broadcast satire into another country with the goal of sowing dissent all throughout the region?

To answer this, let's go back to World War II, where we will meet Bruno Adler, a hero of mine.

It is somewhat ironic that the man who published a book called *Utopia: Documents of Reality* would play a hand in warcraft. But for Bruno Adler, this was just another Tuesday.[98]

Adler was born on Bohemia to Therese and Moritz Adler, the latter of which was an editor for the social democratic newspaper *Volkswille* and an elected representative. As Adler grew up, he became fascinated with the history of literature and art, to the point where he would teach art history at the Weimar Saxon-Grand Ducal Art School for many years.

---

98   Kristina Moorehead, "How Britain Fought Hitler with Humour," *BBC*, August 30, 2019.

That is, until the Nazis seized power. Adler, born to Jewish parents, immediately went into exile in Prague. In
1936, he went to England and began writing under an
anagram of his name: Urban Roedl. His writing made
waves on both sides of the war—especially when he was
picked up by the BBC in England for his great reporting
and storytelling abilities.

He was met there by the Austrian exile and fellow Jew
Robert Lucas. Lucas had left Austria when his party, the
Social Democratic Workers' Party of Austria, was out-
lawed. Knowing that his fate would be sealed if he stayed
in Austria, he emigrated to London in 1934. Having been
a political author in the past, he began work for the Austrian newspaper *Neue Freie Presse* from afar, and he was
picked up by the BBC in 1938 to work for the new German
Service of the BBC.

The goal of the German Service was simple in theory,
yet incredibly complicated in practice: to break the Nazi
monopoly on news within the Third Reich. The Nazis had
made listening to enemy radio stations a crime—but they
could not stop foreign radio waves from crossing into
Germany and being picked up by receivers. The penalty
for listening was severe; those who were caught could
be killed.

Lucas and Adler worked together to broadcast several
programs into Nazi Germany. But they did not write
news about the war, as we might expect. Rather, the BBC
had Lucas and Adler broadcast satire over the radio to
those under occupation.

But why broadcast satire? Shouldn't they have broadcasted the news, or even something like the weather

to gain credibility? Jokes might be a good idea to keep morale up within Britain (as the BBC did with their wartime satire *It's That Man Again*), but why send satire into enemy territory? And, perhaps most importantly, who the hell is going to listen to satire of all things when their life is on the line?

Lucas, Adler, and their bosses at the BBC didn't know the answer to any of these questions, but they tried anyway. When they began writing their first program, *Die Briefe des Gefreiten Adolf Hirnschal (Corporal Adolf Hirnschal's Letters)*, they had no clue if anyone would listen. Lucas would later describe how he had "no idea whether there would be at least fifty people in Germany listening…[We spoke] into the dark without any echo."[99]

Die Briefe des Gefreiten Adolf Hirnschal was a series of fictitious letters written by a German corporal, Adolf Hirnschal, on the front line to his wife. On the surface, Hirnschal is devoted to the "beloved Führer," but he is written as being so loyal that he exposes the paradoxical and dishonest nature of Nazi statements. Take the example from the first 'letter' after the Nazis declared war on Russia in 1941, where Hirnschal tells his wife that he is being transferred to the Russian border:

I jump up in joy and say: 'Mr. Lieutenant, kindly asking for permission to express that I am tremendously pleased that we are now fraternizing with the Russians. Did not our beloved Führer already say in 1939 that our friendship with the Russians is irrevocable and irreversible?'[100]

---

99   Ibid.

100 Charlotte Runcie, "How the BBC Tried to Beat Hitler with Humour—and Why It's so Nice to Hear Some of It in The Archers," *The Telegraph*, September 4, 2019.

How Jokes Can Give Hope to Our Fractured World

Under the cover of complete loyalty, the hypocrisy of Hitler's Russia policy is brought into the limelight. A similar strategy was used by Adler when he wrote a different show, "Frau Wernicke" ("Mrs. Wernicke"). Frau Wernicke is a chatty Berlin housewife who complains about injustices, food rations, and other issues she sees in her everyday life during the war. Her naïve support for Nazism is constantly juxtaposed with the stark realities of war that she experiences. In one show, Frau Wernicke asks her friend why her friend is upset, answering her own question in the process of doing so (note the ironic use of "only" at the beginning):

Only because your husband had to close his business and because your boy is now with the Wehrmacht and has had enough of it and because your girl, Elsbeth, has to do a second mandatory year of state labor and because—as you put it— you don't have a family life anymore and you are not happy?[101]

Adler also wrote "Kurt und Willi" ("Kurt and Willi"), another program that featured a teacher, Kurt Krüger, and an official in the German Ministry of Propaganda, Willi Schimanski. The men are often found discussing the war over a beer, where Kurt, the representation for the average German citizen, is told by Willi all the deceit, tricks, and lies that the Propaganda Ministry utilized. Willi was supposedly so skilled and so truthful that he was admired within the actual Nazi Ministry of Propaganda in Nazi Germany (delightfully called the Reich Ministry of Public Enlightenment and Propaganda). This

101 Jennifer Taylor, "The 'Endsieg as Ever-Receding Goal. Literary Propaganda by Bruno Adler and Robert Lucas for BBC Radio," Essay, In *German-Speaking Exiles in Great Britain* 1. (Amsterdam: Rodopi, 1999), 44–57.

tells us that the Nazis, completely disconnected from the reality of those in their domain, saw the program as educational—but what did the citizens think of them?

The broadcasts lasted through the war, from summer 1940 all the way until the end of the war. The target of these broadcasts is the average person faced with the seemingly never-ending war. Weekly shows hinted at food and clothing shortages, repeatedly reminding the public of the high loss of life at home and on the battlefield. Moreover, the shows highlighted parallels between this conflict and World War I, which ended with Germany in defeat and was fresh in the minds of many Germans. When the Nazis finally understood that some of these shows could be effective propaganda if heard by the public, they tried to jam the signal with music to stop the broadcasts from being audible. The BBC responded by making the sentences shorter so that they could be heard over the music.

Which returns us to the question: was anyone even listening? Any German who would listen disregarded the law, had to be aware of eavesdroppers and their neighborhood Nazi loyalists, and had the prospect of death awaiting them if caught. Any one of those are enough to keep away many people from all sorts of activities—if you wanted a Snickers bar but eating one was illegal and punishable by death, you probably could find another way to satisfy your craving.

But when the war was over, Lucas recalled the "flood of thank-you letters" that he received. The German Services showed ordinary Germans that the British understood them, unlike their Nazi overlords. Within these letters were statements like the following:

The London broadcasts saved me from suicide during the blackest days of the Hitler war.

It's thanks to the BBC and the BBC alone that I had the moral strength not to become complicit.

That you also brought us humor made the unbearable bearable for us.[102]

For everyone else not living under Axis rule, laughing at Hitler both soothed fears and took the Nazis down a few pegs. The shows brought the people within authoritarianism hope. Dictatorships like the Nazis thrive on intimidation and threats. They parade down the street, beat up political opponents, publicly humiliate anyone they deem an enemy of the state, and produce films aimed to show their invulnerability. Making the Nazis look ridiculous lessened the fear of Nazis and also deflated Nazi grandiosity.

Being caught was punishable by imprisonment for treason, but those under occupation believed that the humor was worth the risk.

But most importantly, the broadcasts gave people hope that their situation could change. They were plagued by clothing and food shortages. Life was miserable and some even felt like becoming complicit was the only way to survive. But as these letters show us, through these radio programs, individuals remained hopeful that there was someone fighting for change.

But there is one more aspect of humor as propaganda that must be noted: how humor influences those not in war. Does humor and satire have a role in convincing

---

102 Moorehead, "How Britain Fought Hitler," 2019.

other countries and their citizens that one side is right? That one side are the good guys and the others are selfish, power- and bloodthirsty enemies? That there is hope that the good guys will win and the bad guys will lose?

The answer is a resounding yes.

Take Charlie Chaplin's 1940 satire, *The Great Dictator*, where Chaplin parodies Hitler and the Nazi regime. The film is about a Jewish barber, played by Chaplin, who is mistaken for a certain dictator he resembles and is asked to take his place.

Chaplin and Hitler were extremely similar in background (they were born four days apart in April 1889, and both had risen to great power from a childhood of poverty). Chaplin's son would later write:

Their destinies were poles apart. One was to make millions weep, while the other was to set the whole world laughing. Dad could never think of Hitler without a shudder, half of horror, half of fascination. "Just think," he would say uneasily, "he's the madman, I'm the comic. But it could have been the other way around."[103]

But still, Chaplin chose to shoot the movie, reportedly after his films were banned from Nazi Germany because Hitler thought Chaplin looked a bit too much like him. Another account says that Chaplin wanted to make the film after reading a 1934 anti-Semitic propaganda leaflet that called him a "disgusting Jewish acrobat." (The Nazi's were wrong—Chaplin was raised Protestant and

---

103 Charles Chaplin, N. Rau, and M. Rau, *My Father, Charlie Chaplin.* (London: Panter, 1961).

as an adult did not follow any organized religion—but this mistake made Chaplin laugh.)[104]

The Great Dictator began filming six days after World War II broke out, finishing just six months later. It wasn't the first parody of Hitler in the United States (*You Nazty Spy!* by the Three Stooges claim that title), but it quickly became the most popular movie, even though Chaplin feared that wartime audiences would dislike a comedy about a "fictitious" dictator.

Chaplin would tell his son during production, "I'm praying, son, that this picture will have a good message and maybe help mankind a bit." And help mankind it did.

For audiences in the United States, *The Great Dictator* gave the public hope that the fight they were fighting was a worthwhile effort. The movie made a mockery of Nazism and drastically helped quell American fears about the war. Furthermore, Chaplin's anti-fascist message influenced the US population toward action/interventionism (as opposed to inaction/isolationism, who did not care much about what was going on in Europe and, in isolationist fashion, did not want to take sides between Hitler and those he persecuted).

Perhaps more importantly, humor allowed Chaplin's message to be broadcasted all over the world. At the end of the film, Chaplin delivers a stunning six-minute monologue, where he all but drops character and looks directly at the camera. He cries out, "We think too much and feel too little. More than machinery, we need humanity. More than cleverness, we need kindness and gentleness.

104 Charles Chaplin, *Charles Chaplin: My Autobiography*. (London: The Bodley Head, 1964).

Without these qualities, life will be violent and all will be lost."[105] Film historian Jeffrey Vance would later describe this speech in his book, *Chaplin: Genius of the Cinema*:

Here Chaplin drops his comic mask and speaks directly to the world, conveying his view that people must rise up against dictators and unite in peace. The most enduring aspects of the final speech are its aspirational quality and tone and its underlying faith in humanity. Chaplin sketches a hopeful future in broad strokes and leaves the implementation of his vision to others, despite the fact that the more unsavory aspects of human nature may prevent mankind ever reaching his promised utopia.[106]

Critics at the time hated the scene for being overly sentimental (modern critics have praised it as a historically significant and important work of satire), but the average viewer loved it. Chaplin speaks to all who listened and laughed just a few short minutes beforehand. He looks directly into the camera, right into the viewers' eyes, and tells them that there is hope in the world.

Reportedly, one of those viewers was the Führer himself. A refugee from Germany who worked in the Nazi Ministry of Culture told Chaplin that Hitler had watched *The Great Dictator* not once, but twice. Both times entirely alone. Chaplain replied that he would "give anything to know what he thought of it." I would too.

Fast forward to 2014, where comedians Seth Rogen and Evan Goldberg have just finished wrapping up their next big movie, *The Interview*. *The Interview* featured

---

105 Charlie Chaplin, and Charlie Chaplin, *The Great Dictator*, 1940.

106 Jeffrey Vance, *Chaplin: Genius of the Cinema.* (New York, New York: Harry N. Abrams, 2003).

Seth Rogen and James Franco, journalists who received an opportunity to interview North Korea leader Kim Jong-un, played by Randall Park. Naturally, the CIA gets involved, and all of a sudden Rogen and Franco are key in an assassination plot to kill Kim Jong-un. The film is comical—It was a hilarious premise to all except a select few.

On the morning of November 24, 2014, employees logging onto the Sony Network were shown the terrifying image of a fiery skeleton as gunshots blared from their computers' speakers. The malware leaped from machine to machine, destroying everything in its process. It erased 48 percent of Sony's nearly seven thousand personal computers, and destroyed over 50 percent of their servers. When finished erasing, the code fried each computer's start-up software. Within minutes, the Sony office was reduced to fax machines and paper checks—not ideal for one of the top electronics companies in the world. Over the next three weeks, the hackers dumped batches of confidential files onto public file-sharing websites. Internal (and sometimes gossipy) e-mail, more than forty-seven thousand Social Security numbers, several unreleased movies, and more were available for free viewing by anyone who wanted to see them.[107]

Less than a month later, the FBI blamed the attack on North Korea, which had already issued threats over the film itself. (Note: the official attacker was a group that goes by the name "Guardians of Peace," but the FBI has established the connection to North Korea.) North Korea even threatened a "9/11 attack" against theaters that chose to show the film.

---

107 Peter Elkind, "Sony Pictures: Inside the Hack of the Century," *Fortune*, June 27, 2019.

But why would a country get so mad at a few comedians making fun of their leader? Feelings of offense make sense, but hostile actions for a movie where Seth Rogen shoves a cucumber-sized capsule up his tuchus seems over the top.

Perhaps we can find an answer in Jang Jin-sung, a former state-appointed North Korean poet laureate who defected to South Korea just over a decade ago. In North Korea, he was a psychological warfare expert with the role of crafting pro-regime propaganda and developing epic poetry promoting Kim Jong-un's father, the late Kim Jong-il. Jin-sung isn't just some defector, he's the perfect North Korean defector to discuss the North Korean response to *The Interview*.

As Jung said in a recent interview, "From the North Korean's point of view, it's as explosive as if a real bomb were dropped on Kim Jong-un. It's a cultural bomb. And it has nothing to do with the story or the presentation or the acting—or really with the movie itself. It's just the notion that Kim Jong-un can be assassinated in a film. It's so shocking. It's beyond-the-pale blasphemous." North Korean leaders cement their power by constantly and relentlessly insisting that its leader is infallible—a concept satirized by Rogen and Goldberg beyond belief in the film.

While North Koreans don't necessarily believe that their leader is a god, Jung notes, "In the North Korean system, you have to praise Kim and sing hymns about him and take it seriously...It's not that people are brainwashed and think he's God. These are things that people know, but that they don't dare to challenge. Where the movie is really powerful is that it comes from the outside, and does the exact opposite. That's where the magic is." Jung highlights the need for what he called "low-brow and dirty-humored" movies. He elaborates:

It was quite a bad film, actually, quite silly and stupid. But conversely, if the same movie had been made better—more serious and more crafted—it might have actually made things worse in North Korea, because it might have made North Korea look more powerful. But it's just a toilet humor movie. And the fact that North Korea feels it's inappropriate to make, it just undermines the cult even further. That's cool! [Laughs][108]

The question quickly becomes, why humor? Why does humor have such powerful effects, ones that Jung thinks could potentially disrupt the entire authoritarian regime?

It's because in humor there is truth. Think about how we've talked about reframing issues using humor—how Lily Rickman made it appear like the Nazi guards were working for her. A joke works when it forces us to consider another worldview. ("Oh, there really is a reason why a chicken would cross a road. How ridiculous!") In the case of a people who have been fed lies about their rulers day in and day out, a joke at the Glorious Leader's expense offers a window into another world—one where their ruler might not be as divine as he's made himself out to be.

---

108 Katie Engelhart, "Former North Korean Poet Laureate Says 'The Interview' Is As Explosive As a Real Bomb Being Dropped on Kim Jong-Un," *VICE*, January 2, 2015.

10

The North Korean Jokester

___

It's 1960. The British prime minister, Harold Macmillan, is addressing the United Nations. The world is watching and holding onto every word, as the international debate between capitalism and communism rages on all over the world.

But Nikita Khrushchev, the Soviet leader, was having none of it. He stood up abruptly, shouting and hammering on his desk (some say with his own shoe), drawing the attention of everyone watching.

Prime Minister Macmillan paused and said, "I'd like that translated, if I may."

I understand that on the page it's not such a great joke. But in the UN chamber, world leaders howled with laughter. Khrushchev sat down.[109]

Diplomats and world leaders are faced with some of the most difficult tasks known to mankind: they represent and protect their home nations, they facilitate strategic

___

109 "Humour and Diplomacy." *Diplomat Magazine*, February 5, 2018.

agreements and treaties, and they ensure friendly relations between countries.

In the words of one diplomatic correspondent, "They are the people who can tell you to go to hell in a way that makes you ask for directions; the honest men and women sent abroad to lie for the good of their country; the officials who can step on someone's toes without spoiling the shine of their shoes."[110]

Undoubtedly, humor is helpful to the practice of diplomacy by encouraging others to accept a diplomat's offers. As the comedian John Cleese explains, "If I can get you to laugh with me, you like me better, which makes you more open to my ideas. And if I can persuade you to laugh at the particular point I make, by laughing at it, you acknowledge the truth."[111]

The Irish playwright Bernard Shaw was a bit blunter: "If you are going to tell people the truth, you better make them laugh; otherwise, they'll kill you."[112]

Humor is akin to adding a little bit of sugar to the harsh words that diplomats are often charged with delivering. In 2017, European foreign ministers had a tense meeting with the Burmese national security advisor over the Burmese treatment of the Rohingya. This was not supposed to be a pleasant meeting. However, one diplomat displayed such geniality and humor that it was near-impossible for the Burmese official to walk out in a huff.[113]

---

110 Ibid.

111 Nicki Joy, Essay, In *What Winners Do To Win: The 7 Minutes a Day That Can Change Your Life.* (Hoboken, NJ: John Wiley & Sons, 2003), 113.

112 Kevin Willmott, Director, 2004, *C.S.A.: The Confederate States of America.* Hodcarrier Films, 2004.

113 "Humour", *Diplomat Magazine*, 2018.

How Jokes Can Give Hope to Our Fractured World

However, such tense meetings are not as common as we think. We also need to understand how comedy is used in the daily life of a diplomat.

Meet Sigríður Ásdís Snævarr. Sigríður Ásdís Snævarr is a warrior. When she joined the Icelandic foreign service in 1978, she didn't start off with any small assignment—she went to the Soviet Union at the height of the Cold War. (This would be her first deployment, as she would later serve as Iceland's ambassador to Sweden, Finland, Estonia, Latvia, Slovenia, Namibia, South Africa, Mozambique, France, Italy, Spain, and Portugal, to name a few.) She was young, only twenty-six, and she remembers living in absolute horror. Every time she ventured out of the Icelandic Embassy, Snævarr was scared that she would be arrested by Soviet authorities—and she had no idea what would come after getting arrested.

So, what did she and her fellow diplomats do? They made jokes. "We had so many good jokes. And I remember some of us saying that we should actually put a statue up for humor because it kept you going." This is a theme we have seen and will see repeatedly: that when in trouble, it is best to joke.

Even when not in life-threatening situations, there are key reasons for humor in the diplomatic world. Humor has a way of allowing all involved to lower their guard. However, relationships are key in the diplomatic world, even when the two countries that the diplomats represent are not in conflict.

When Snævarr was invited to one diplomatic function, she knew no one. She had only been in the region for just over a week when the Icelandic embassy received an invitation to an "enormous reception."

I had no idea who anyone was...I've never felt as lonely. I had made a courtesy call on some of the Nordics but they were not there or I couldn't find them among the eleven hundred people there. I remember what I did—I went to where the food was, loitered around the food, waiting for someone to come and just chat about anything. You can imagine that in a situation like that, just saying a joke or saying something jovial. It's exactly breaking the ice, as you say in English, and we say that in Icelandic. It's the same in French and also in German (Snævarr speaks eight languages). So, it's an interesting thing that exists in all these languages...But I saw a very strange woman next to me, with very yellow hair. I say to her, "Can you imagine that I have been here for ten days and I am in front of eleven hundred people and I know no one?"

Notice how Snævarr poked fun at herself—not at anyone else at the function or at the Nordics who did not show up. By poking fun at herself, she excellently displays that she is letting her own shields down, thus inviting her fellow diplomat to do the same.

But Snævarr hinted at another key reason all diplomats need humor:

I remember the diplomats who I really looked up to. They would be storytellers, really. And there is one definition of a good ambassador. They are a storyteller and a tour guide.

A key aspect of storytelling, for Snævarr, is ensuring that the audience has a good time listening to the person telling the story. A good diplomat can get by without humor; a great diplomat wields humor constantly. While there is such a thing as a story without humor, humorous storytelling for a diplomat is a necessary tool for building a rapport between their counterparts and their enemies.

This leads us to the strange story of a North Korean diplomat. North Korea as a nation is infamous for its lack of a sense of humor, but the diplomat could joke with the best of them. In the words of one academic who encountered him, "It was enough to change one's entire mind-set about the 'Hermit Nation' and its diplomats." When the North Korean and the academic were both at a dinner together after a conference, the North Korean diplomat raised his glass in a toast to President Bush, saying that "with relations between the two of us improving so rapidly, [he'd] soon have to find housing when [the North Korean] embassy opened in Washington."[114]

The North Korean diplomat would later say that he once met with President Bush—a claim ridiculous to the American diplomats who knew that meetings between the two countries were non-existent, even at the desk officer level due to no formal relations between the two countries. The North Korean diplomat proceeded to pull out his wallet and, with a cunning smile, showed his fellow diplomats a photo of himself with his arm around a smiling President Bush directly in front of the White House. Of course, it was the cardboard figure of the President, causing laughter to arise from all around the table. This humor did wonders for the relationships between the diplomats.[115]

---

114 Gene Schmiel, "Humor in the Foreign Service: Not Necessarily an Oxymoron," *American Diplomacy*, April 1999.

115 Ibid.

Any tensions in the room were immediately eased. In the words of one South Korean diplomat, "The sense of humor is an indispensable resource for diplomats, who work in the first line of intercultural contact, because intelligent humor often serves as a lubricant that helps to reduce the frictions caused by the lack of mutual understanding."[116]

Without humor, our hope of being an interconnected world becomes harder and harder to manifest. The reason why humor gives hope in the diplomatic sphere is that, even in conflict, it is a reminder of why countries have diplomats: to hope for a better future for their country. When diplomats make jokes with each other, they are able to maintain hope that together they can overcome whatever challenges come their way. After all, jokes are best made in good company, and to joke with another is to signal that you are comfortable with them—or at the very least, are trying to become more comfortable with them. In the diplomatic sphere, this is critical. If there is no hope of working together for a better future, or that there is a solution to global problems, what's the point in working together at all?

Sometimes diplomats cross a rather important line. It's not easy to understand the jokes of other cultures—so when one diplomat makes a joke that doesn't translate well, there can be dangerous consequences. The United Kingdom Prime Minister Boris Johnson is notorious for his humor, but with great power comes great responsibility. At a reception where Prime Minister Johnson was

116 Alberto Rubio, "Sense of Humour Is an Indispensable Resource for Diplomats," The Diplomat in Spain, January 27, 2018.

How Jokes Can Give Hope to Our Fractured World

meant to welcome foreign ambassadors, he declared: "We have invaded, defeated, or conquered most of your countries, but we are here as friends."[117]

Those in the audience gasped—it wasn't the best joke for the crowd, since it was a classic example of humor in bad taste—where the powerful (the former colonizer) makes a joke about the less powerful (the former colonies). Naturally, it failed, but this event serves as an important lesson for all of those who engage with others, even outside the international political sphere: avoid mocking their predicaments, especially if you or who you represent caused the predicaments!

***

Importantly, all of the prior examples are reliant upon some international institution already being in place— usually the United Nations, but sometimes other international organizations like NATO. So, if we take those away, what's to happen?

Let's journey back to the Vietnam War, where one of my idols, the diplomat Henry Kissinger, is working with his counterpart in the North Vietnamese government, Lê Đức Thọ. The Vietnam War had been waged for nearly fifteen years and had taken the lives of millions. Time was of the essence; as they spoke, bombs rained down over North Vietnam.

The world was solemn, but the room was full of laughter. Why?

117 Ibid.

Let's take one example, where Thọ had requested that, after the agreement was signed, the US would not continue its military involvement in the region. A fairly simple ask, sure, but doing so would require the deletion of a clause that allowed US troops to stay in the region for up to sixty days post-ceasefire. Kissinger replied to the request, "You won't let us interfere for sixty days more?" Laughter ensued.[118]

After the laughter subsided, Thọ retorted, "So you want to continue to interfere for sixty days more?" Kissinger responded: "It is a habit that is so hard to break." More laughter. Kissinger would eventually leave that section of the agreement vague, allowing both sides to remain in the area post-ceasefire. The conversation put the two on a plane of mutual respect, where both were able to tell the other what they wanted without hostility—thus allowing them to come to a conclusion amicably.

McMaster University researcher Harish C. Mehta reviewed all the transcripts of these conversations between Kissinger and Thọ, and in his work, *Fighting, Negotiating, Laughing: The Use of Humor in the Vietnam War*, he notes how in the official record of the meetings, there are several times when the negotiators laughed at each other's comments. In fact, laughter is the only emotion written into the official record of the meetings. No anger, no hostility, not even a mention of calmness, but laughter.

Kissinger joked, "If we can't find every [North Vietnamese] tank, we are not likely to find every soldier."

---

118 Harish C. Mehta, "Fighting, Negotiating, Laughing: The Use of Humor in the Vietnam War," *The Historian* 74, no. 4 (January 10, 2012): 743–88.

Everyone laughed, then Thọ quipped, "You can't find them because all of them are Vietnamese." More laughter. Thọ's response highlighted a serious issue the US was having in the south: North Vietnamese soldiers could seamlessly merge with common villagers, making it nearly impossible for American soldiers to identify who was who. It was guerilla warfare, and it made it difficult for the United States to fight against them.[119]

The American writer Dwight Macdonald once observed that humor is like guerrilla warfare because success depends on traveling light, striking unexpectedly, and getting away fast.[120] The North Vietnamese were the embodiment and the evidence of such a comparison.

For both parties at the table, humor served an essential and positive purpose. For Kissinger, his jokes were usually an acknowledgement of the power that the North Vietnamese had in some scenarios over the United States (see the Vietnamese tank joke a few paragraphs ago). Sometimes, though, Kissinger's jokes were a show of American power in the world at large (see the joke about the habits of the US military). For Thọ, humor was used to demonstrate and illustrate their resistance to US power in the region. By making a joke, the North Vietnamese could highlight an issue they took with the United States without any explicit hostility that could potentially delineate any. The North Vietnamese showed their steadfast resilience in their ability to laugh at the enemy—and because they joked, they showed that they still had hope for themselves. As we know, those who can

---

119 Ibid.

120 Dwight Macdonald, *On Movies* (Englewood Cliffs, New Jersey: Da Capo Press, 1981).

still laugh and joke are rarely devoid of all hope. Notice how humor is a weapon here in addition to a tool.

In total, humor built a rapport between the two feuding countries. It was as if both countries were saying, "Yes, we can joke about this, and because we can joke with each other, we can come to an agreement about our differences." Even at the height of a bloody conflict, it was humor that kept spirits alive and driving toward the conclusion of the war.

11

Funny Guy

———

This past winter, I was fortunate enough to stay over-
night in Atlanta, Georgia. While this may sound trivial,
almost inconsequential, to many, I was interested in only
one thing: the commercials. See, the SEC Championship
was being played on nearly every television in sight; but
as someone who couldn't tell you what the difference is
between a safety and a cornerback, I waited patiently for
each touchdown and break—because I knew that after
those, I would be getting commercials for the upcoming
Senate run-off races between Democratic candidates Jon
Ossoff and Rev. Raphael Warnock and Republican incum-
bents Sen. David Perdue and Sen. Kelly Loeffler.

The race would decide which party had control over the
Senate, and as such, millions of dollars were being put
into advertising between touchdowns of one of the most
watched college football games of the season. What did
Rev. Warnock do? He ran a thirty-second ad with the
following opening:

Raphael Warnock eats pizza with a fork and knife.

Raphael Warnock once stepped on a crack in the sidewalk.

Raphael Warnock even hates puppies.[121]

Following these claims, Rev. Warnock appears on the screen, advising those in the Peach State to watch out for his opponents' attack ads because, according to Rev. Warnock, they only serve to "try and scare you with lies about me...And for the record, I love puppies."

Those around me at the hotel laughed at the last line—one guy in a Clemson shirt next to me laughed and said, "Funny guy"—showing that in my extremely limited sample, humor had a role in elections. It's impossible to know if the humorous advertisements had a causal impact on his win—but they most certainly did not hurt.

But my question becomes, does this translate over into international affairs? What happens when politicians use humor concerning war, or conflict, or international agreements?

Based on what I've discovered, there are two reasons why politicians and heads of state need to use humor to be more effective in dealing with international crises: domestic and international.

Humor from a head of state does two things in the domestic sphere: First, it helps heads of state appear more likable and trustworthy. Take, for example, George W. Bush's appearance on *The Late Show* in 2000. According to some recent analysis, Bush's interview with host David Letterman allowed people to get to know Bush as an individual, beyond just his policies and his stump speeches. He was trustworthy and likable. In the end, viewers who

121 "Reverend Raphael Warnock: 'Get Ready' | Campaign 2020," *The Washington Post*, November 5, 2020.

saw Bush's appearance on the show were more likely to believe that he "really cares about people like me."[122] When spearheading your country into international conflict, it's critical for the voting populous to truly believe that the politician is doing so in the best interest of the people—and if some gentle ribbing on a late-night television show is what is necessary to help convince the public of such, comedy serves as a wonderfully efficient tool for politicians to appear more trustworthy.

Second, humor quells fears about any particular issue. It is important to note here that humor does not alleviate a particular course of action; rather, it attacks any opposition that may be coming their way; it takes the effectiveness out of an opponent's jab. For example, let's say in a hypothetical world that a young leader is being blasted by older politicians for invading a country on the grounds of human rights atrocities taking place in that country. What would work better between the two following options: a fifteen-minute-long segment during a presidential address combatting each point in detail, or a one-liner about the changing times of politics and how we don't just invade for oil anymore.

While hypothetical, there are a few reasons to opt for the humorous one-liner. First, it's more memorable. Much like many of former US President Ronald Reagan's one-liners, it can be spread both in person-to-person conversation and through the internet far easier than an elongated speech. Second, when the average person's attention span is roughly eight seconds long, it's far, far more likely

---

122 Patricia Moy, Michael A. Xenos, and Verena K. Hess, "Priming Effects of Late-Night Comedy," *International Journal of Public Opinion Research* 18, no. 2 (July 22, 2005): 198–210.

that someone will pay attention to (and remember) the one-liner than each and every point made in the extensive rebuttal option.

As a real example of this, US President Abraham Lincoln was often bashed by his critics for being two-faced. In one debate with the Democratic challenger Stephen A. Douglas, Douglas accused Lincoln point-blank of being two-faced. Lincoln could have responded via an extensive speech on how he was in fact not two-faced, rather, Douglas just didn't understand what it took to be a president in a time of civil unrest.

Instead, Lincoln responded with one of my favorite lines from presidential debate history: "Honestly, if I were two-faced, would I be showing you this one?"[123]

Brilliant. In just twelve words, Lincoln disarms Douglas and makes the audience laugh—which, as we know, also helps Lincoln's likeability and trustworthiness.

As an extension of this concept, political leaders can use humor to deflect criticism from the media—whose very job is often to try and criticize political leaders. President Dwight Eisenhower was notoriously good at this. Eisenhower, whose brother Edgar was a vocal critic of the President, once had the following answer during a news conference:

Q: Your brother Edgar is in the news this morning for voicing some criticism about your budget and the general direction your administration is taking. He also says he is disturbed about the liberal influence of Milton and Sherm Adams. Do you have any comment?

123 Robert Mankoff, "Lincoln's Smile," *The New Yorker*, June 19, 2017.

President Eisenhower: Edgar has been criticizing me since I was five years old.[124]

The transcript then says "[Laughter]," showing that the whole room was appeased by such an answer.[125] Notice how Eisenhower doesn't even touch on the criticism about his administration or about any influence coming from outside the administration.

Similar to Eisenhower, US President Bill Clinton used humor to reframe his election results:

Q: Mr. President, this is twice now you've been elected with less than 50 percent of the vote. How big of a disappointment was that to you, and is that going to hamstring you now?

President Clinton: Not much. The 379 electoral votes was an enormous consolation prize.[126]

President Clinton both accepts the outcome of the election with regards to the popular vote, but entirely reframes such an issue to look at the Electoral College— which gave Clinton the electoral victory. All this while the journalists in the room laughed at his reframing of the issue.

Critically, this reframing isn't limited to just domestic political issues, but with regards to international crises as well. Take as our example President Bush when asked about the possibility that the US goes to war with Iraq:

---

124 Dick M. Carpenter, Marjory J. Webster, and Chad K. Bowman, "White House Wit: How Presidents Use Humor as a Leadership Tool," *Presidential Studies Quarterly* 49, no. 1 (January 8, 2019): 23–55.

125 Office of the Federal Register, and Dwight D. Eisenhower, Public Papers of the Presidents of the United States § (1953).

126 "Excerpts From Remarks by Clinton at His Post-Election News Conference," *The New York Times*, November 9, 1996.

Q: Mr. President, I've been out in the country on vacation, and a lot of people have asked me, "What are the chances that we're actually going to war with Iraq?" I mean, how likely is war, and what would trigger it?

President Bush: Right. That's the question that you should ask to [Iraqi President] Saddam Hussein.[127]

Laughter ensued once again.

Look at what President Bush does here: first, he reframes the war itself as not something the United States will be propagating; rather, the Iraqi government will be the ones to decide whether or not a war occurs. As such, Bush makes it appear as if he is the good guy in the international system, as opposed to the Iraqi President Saddam Hussein. When trying to convince the international system to join your efforts, it's definitely a good thing to be seen as the guy forced into going to war as opposed to the one instigating it.

This is the second arena where humor serves an immense purpose for political leaders: the international political sphere. We saw with the example above how humor can be used to reframe conflict—that is, to make it clear that the United States sees itself as launching a defensive war as opposed to invading another country. In the international system, it's critical for them to do so to make sure that other countries support, or at the very least don't oppose, US action.

Moreover, many of the lessons we learned from the diplomats last chapter apply to heads of state. First off, humor helps build relationships between heads of state,

---

127 "President Meets with Leaders of Kenya and Ethiopia," National Archives and Records Administration, December 5, 2002.

which is critical for making the relationship between countries stronger. Second, heads of state function as top diplomats, meaning that humor is a wonderful way to help work through issues between countries, much like Kissinger and Thọ did in the last chapter. Finally, political leaders are able to establish continued relationships with other political leaders—which bodes well for the future of their respective countries.

PART IV

12

The Most Dangerous Phrase

———

Up until this point in the book, I've been treating humor as a universally good thing—and for nearly every instance we've looked at so far, it is—but just because something is funny doesn't necessarily mean that it is good or beneficial to the international system. We'll explore what I see as the two biggest places where comedy and humor are used to exclude or indoctrinate, but in reality, it all boils down to what I believe is the most dangerous phrase in the international lexicon:

"I was just joking."

To explore this idea further, we are going to travel back to 1930s Ottoman Palestine (now-Israel), where German Jews, called Yekkes, were immigrating. The joke goes a little like this:

A young man, newly arrived from Germany in the late 1930s, recognizes a former teacher on the street in Tel Aviv. Coming abreast, the young man greets the older one with all of the old-world honorifics at his command. "Herr Professor, Doktor," he begins. Responding with pleasure, but conscious of the incongruity, the professor replies, "This is an egalitarian country, my son. Just call me adonai."[128]

Because I'm assuming most of those reading this book don't understand Hebraic puns, I'll explain: Adonai, in Hebrew, means "God." Adoni, on the other hand, means "master," the equivalent of "sir" at the time. It is one of roughly one hundred fifty jokes told.

These jokes are an example of ethnic humor, which we will define as "humor directed at, and typically at the expense of, nationality groups."[129] They are based on ethnic stereotypes and other shared beliefs about certain ethnic groups. There is a necessary differentiation here between other-depreciating and self-deprecating humor. Members of dominant and powerful ethnic groups tend to tell jokes only about other groups (and rarely are self-deprecating). Because they enforce the power structure that benefits the dominant group, ethnic humor serves as a control mechanism. The joke above serves as an example of this: by joking about the Yekkes' inability to speak the language, the joke serves as a social pressure to get the Yekkes to assimilate into the culture.

Ethnic humor is where jokes go bad. It entrenches negative stereotypes of the other while simultaneously creating a sense of solidarity and superiority among the 'in-group,' such as the group with the dominant language. Particularly in a nation-state after a large flux

128 Limor Shifman, and Elihu Katz, "Just Call Me Adonai: A Case Study of Ethnic Humor and Immigrant Assimilation," *American Sociological Review* 70 (October 2005): 843–59.

129 Ibid.

of immigrants where ethnic jokes serve as an elusive means of social control, they are a message that carries an implicit call for laughter against a "different" group.

Limor Shifman and Elihu Katz, two professors from Oxford and the University of Pennsylvania respectively, suggest "ethnic humor may carry a dual message of "welcome to our melting pot, but notice that it is our ethnicity (and superiority) that defines this nation.""[130]

Let's explore this concept through the aforementioned Yekkes. But to fully understand the situation (and the jokes themselves), we must understand a few historical precursors to the migration. Up until the eighteenth century, Eastern/Polish and Western/Germanic Jews were not needing of such a differentiation—through the active exchange of rabbis/scholars and the repeated involvement in each other's affairs. However, throughout the eighteenth century, social gaps developed between the two groups. German Jews were entering new occupational fields and interacting with Christian populations, whereas severe restrictions on Polish Jews created an isolated Jewish life with few occupational opportunities.

When Jews were forced to flee from Eastern Europe to Germany in the latter half of the eighteenth century, German Jews, to quote one scholar, welcomed them as "brothers and strangers."[131] The Polish Jews were labeled Ostjuden and were considered by the German Jews as backward, dirty, and uncivilized. As a result, the German Jews saw their Polish counterparts as a detriment to the

---

130 Ibid.

131 Steven E. Aschheim, *Brothers and Strangers: the East European Jew in German and Jewish Consciousness*, 1800-1923. Madison, WI: University of Wisconsin Press, 1982.

progress of German Jewry. Satirical newspapers, which employed many German Jews, mocked the Ostjuden—with the German Jews often joining in on the action.

Near the turn of the century, many Jews from Eastern Europe emigrated to Ottoman Palestine. A rapid increase in population had created economic problems that affected Jewish societies throughout Eastern Europe, leading many Jews to migrate to Ottoman Palestine out of a connection to the land of their ancestors.

The story of Western and Eastern Jewry brings us to the 1930s. World War II had caused over sixty thousand German Jews to emigrate to Ottoman Palestine—the majority of which were relatively wealthy and educated.[132] However, despite their advanced education, many German Jews were "societally downgraded;" for example, doctors suddenly became laborers and lawyers taught themselves to be taxi drivers.

The immigrant German Jews became Yekkes, after their short jackets (called "yekkes") that differentiated from the long coats of the traditional Eastern Europeans who had emigrated decades before. The new term illustrates the perceived uniqueness of the group—marking them as "different" from everyone else.

Limor Shifman and Elihu Katz identified approximately one hundred fifty "Yekke Jokes," most of which come from the joke books of those times. Joke books serve an interesting role in the study of humor—since they are created primarily for commercial purposes, they are designed to appeal to mass audiences and therefore

---

132 "Refugees," In *The Holocaust Encyclopedia*, Washington, D.C.: United States Holocaust Memorial Museum, n.d.

likely represent the stereotypes and attitudes of the time the book was written.

Eastern European Jews, although not known for their rigidity, were known for their sense of humor. They took advantage of their hegemonic position to make Yekkes the butt of their jokes—particularly through their stereotyping of Yekkes as rigid, as opposed to the trait that is the pride of Israel: improvisation. As one joke goes:

A Yekke family wins a refrigerator in the lottery. When the delivery service rings the doorbell at two o'clock in the afternoon, the lady of the house opens the door wearing a robe and refuses to accept the delivery because it has arrived in the Schlafstunde, the daily hour of rest when no disturbance is permitted.[133]

If the stereotypical German Jew (e.g. the Yekke) was polite and civilized, their antithesis was the Israelis, who were self-stereotyped as strong, rough, simple, and sturdy. As Shifman and Katz theorize, "The mockery of the Yekkes, therefore, can be read as an expression of the Israeli attempt to redirect their thinking and behavior, to urge them to trade in their inappropriate personalities and value."

The Yekke jokes can be characterized as corrective humor; that is, they highlight the social borders between Eastern and Western Jews in the Ottoman Palestine while also, in the long term, they might work to lower these same borders by "encouraging" the assimilation of the Yekkes.

According to stereotypes, Yekkes were not just rigid in the realm of mannerisms, but also rigid in mind, or as

133 Schifman et al. "Just Call Me Adonai," *American Sociological Review.*

Shifman and Katz define it, "ostensible stupidity." The most classic of these jokes is below:

A Yekke was asked, "How many eggs can you eat on an empty stomach?" The Yekke ponders a while, and answers, "Two eggs." His questioner chides him, saying, "After one egg, your stomach is no longer empty." Amused, the Yekke returns home and puts the riddle to his wife. The wife answers, "Three eggs," to which the Yekke remorsefully says, "Too bad. If you had answered 'two eggs,' I could have told you a good joke."[34]

The Yekkes' mind is stereotypically ritualistic, so he can only tell the joke in the fashion it was initially said to him, thus missing the point. This theme is also present in a semi-serious explanation that the Hebrew letters to spell the name Yekke is an acronym for "slow-witted Jew" (yehudi kshe havana). Since the Yekkes were notoriously intelligent and well-educated, these jokes were less based on Yekke stereotypes and probably more based on the collective memory of the Eastern European Jews. "Laughter about Yekkes, therefore, may be treated as the sweet 'revenge' of the Ostjuden."

This rigidity may be the reason the Yekkes never learned the Hebrew language, which gave rise to the next topic of Yekke jokes: language.

A Yekke calls for help from a stormy sea that was overwhelming him. He cries, "Hoshiu, hoshiu," which is Hebrew for "save me." A fellow Yekke, walking along the beach, replies to the drowning man, "If you had spent your time learning how to swim instead of learning Hebrew, you'd be a lot better off."[35]

---

134 Ibid.

135 Ibid.

Inviting us to mock the Yekke accent, these jokes often poked fun of the Yekkes' inability to speak Hebrew. They depict immigrant groups as having a marginal identity, if any identity at all. They no longer belong to their original country, but they are not yet absorbed into the new country. In Israel, immigrants were expected to speak only Hebrew and abandon their native language—in a way, these language-centric jokes functioned as a way to enforce the norm of speaking proper Hebrew.

A second variation on culture-based jokes involved the Yekkes' existence as a "nation within a nation." The Yekkes had congregated within a few cities such as Nahariya and certain neighborhoods in Harifa, Jerusalem, and Tel Aviv due to the difficulties they had being absorbed into Israeli society.

Anxiety was provoked in a Yekke community over the news, in 1947, that the United Nations was planning to partition Palestine. Seeking comfort, the community consulted one of its prominent members for the inside story. "Don't worry," he said. "Nahariya (a predominantly Yekke city) will remain German."[136]

Another example of the alienation theme is the young daughter of a Yekke family opening the door for a census-taker and calling out, "Papa, the man from Israel is here again." These jokes created an "us against them" mentality, both psychologically and, to some extent, geographically as well.

The final group of jokes highlights the Yekkes' deference to authority; that is, extreme obedience to the point of blind acceptance without attention paid to ever-changing circumstances (especially in Ottoman Palestine) that may require some level of disobedience.

136 Ibid.

A Yekke feels uncomfortable on the train because the seat he has been assigned is facing in the wrong direction. After he recounts his plight to a (non-Yekke) friend, the friend asks, "Why didn't you ask one of the other passengers to exchange seats with you?" To which the Yekke replies, "I was the only one in the car. There was nobody to ask."[37]

These jokes direct their hearers to make fun of the Yekkes' blind obedience. As Shifman and Katz explain, "In the Israeli context, they might be read as 'corrective' jokes, which try to 'teach' the Yekkes to forgo some of their respect for authority (in this case, the British mandate)."

There is little room for doubt about who or what these jokes are targeted toward. Notably, each of the characteristics scorned in them is correctable; that is, they are not unchangeable features such as intelligence. The majority of jokes, as a result, were to enforce the ideology of the dominant group on the minority group, i.e. the Yekkes. They are as if to say, "be like us," but the implicit notion of that statement is "don't be yourself." Humor can play an effective role in downplaying negative behavior—such as mocking someone who litters—but it crosses the line when it forces the victim to reconsider and drastically change their identity, as seen here.

The two largest groups to arrive after the establishment of Israel as a state (and the spread of English as a dominant language) were the Moroccans and the Russians. The Yekke jokes, like swing dancing and zoot suits, fell out of fashion in favor of jokes about the new waves of immigrants. The Moroccans were the victims of similar

---

137 Ibid.

jokes, such as the following, which enforces the idea that all Moroccans must learn English, the "modern" language:

A senior Israeli politician of Moroccan origin, in exasperation, called the technician to fix his toaster oven, explaining that he had inserted the chicken and pressed the "off" button and nothing happened. (The term "off" is Hebrew for "chicken.")

The Russian immigrants experienced similar jokes to the Yekkes, that is, while Israeli culture was becoming more prosperous, Russians were stereotyped as drunk and promiscuous:

Question: How many Russians does it take to change a light bulb?

Answer: Ten. One holds the bulb and the other nine wait until the vodka makes the room spin.[138]

Generally, the story of the Yekkes, and subsequently the Moroccans and the Russians, teaches us that dominant groups utilize humor to mock minority groups in the process of immigrant assimilation, perhaps to speed up the assimilation process. Another explanation is general anti-immigrant sentiment; while outright racism and xenophobia are often not looked upon fondly within societies, jokes are a somewhat socially acceptable way to express hostile sentiments.

After all, the worst that can happen is the following conversation:

*Person A: *Racist/anti-immigrant joke**

Person B: Hey, that's not cool!

Person A: I was just joking.

---

138 Ibid.

With the "just joking" defense, boundaries are tested within social groups. However, the "just joking" defense is also a way to attempt to escape punishment for crossing the social boundary lines. It can be posited that the "just joking" argument doesn't just avoid blame; it reassigns it. Instead of listeners reprimanding a speaker who says something insensitive, listeners are told they are being overly sensitive for taking offense. These jokes are a form of prejudice that American psychologist Gordon Allport dubbed antilocution.[139] Antilocution focuses on negative verbal remarks made against a group or community, but are not addressed directly to the target of the joke. As a result, the very groups that are the butt of the joke have no clue they are being made fun of. The discrimination is entrenched within society without minority groups even knowing of the change.

Remarks that are intended to make others laugh through the putting down or belittlement of a given target such as social groups belong to a subset of humor called disparagement humor. Disparagement humor both diminishes and reinterprets the butt of the joke. Combine this with the fact that humor communicates its message in a non-serious manner, and we have a unique tool for denigration—one that stifles challenge or criticism.

There are two theories as to why this is the case. The first theory is called psychoanalytic theory, as popularized by Sigmund Freud way back in 1905. Freud theorized that the veiled purpose of such hostile humor is to attack an adversary. In his words, "By making our enemy small, inferior, despicable, or comic, we achieve in

---

139 Gordon W. Allport, *The Nature of Prejudice*. (Reading, MA: Addison-Wesley Pub. Co., 1979.)

a roundabout way the enjoyment of overcoming him."[140] In classic Freudian fashion, disparagement humor provides the joke-maker with a benign way of expressing and satisfying impulses that may otherwise be socially unacceptable. The theory goes a bit further, stating that people enjoy disparagement humor because it provides a release of aggression toward certain groups of people.

The other main theory concerning disparagement humor is superiority theory. As the name suggests, amusement from humor comes from the enhancement of self-esteem derived from looking down upon others. The philosopher Thomas Hobbes explicitly stressed the importance of self-esteem enhancement that results from observing the disparagement of others:

Sudden glory is the passion which maketh those grimaces called laughter, and is caused either by some sudden act of their own, that pleaseth them; or by the apprehension of some deformed thing in another, by comparison whereof they suddenly applaud themselves.[141]

University of Georgia professor Charles Gruner expounds upon this idea, likening disparagement humor to that of a sports competition that involves both conflict that keeps tensions high and a conclusion that results in victory for the winner and defeat for the loser:

When we find humor in something, we laugh at the misfortune, stupidity, clumsiness, moral or cultural defect, suddenly revealed in someone else, to whom we instantly and

---

140 Sigmund Freud and James Strachey, *Jokes and Their Relation to the Unconscious: 1905*. (London: Vintage, 2001).

141 R.E. Ewin, "Hobbes on Laughter," *The Philosophical Quarterly* 51, no. 202 (January 2001): 29–40.

momentarily feel "superior" since we are not, at that moment, unfortunate, stupid, clumsy, morally or culturally defective and so on. To feel superior in this way is "to feel good"; it is to "get what you want." It is to win![142]

Critically, superiority theory doesn't only apply to individuals making fun of other individuals, but also to groups making fun of other groups. The idea is that a person should experience such a self-esteem enhancement upon the disparagement of people or groups that they have no connection with; that is, they will have no empathy for the misfortunate. In 1934, Harvard psychologists tested this theory and found fascinating results. Naturally, non-Jews were more amused than Jews by jokes that disparaged Jews. However, Jews were less amused than non-Jews by anti-Scottish jokes, a common brand of humor at the time.

The Harvard psychologists theorized that because Jewish participants felt sympathy for the Scots, they found the anti-Scottish jokes less amusing. The jokes themselves emphasized and highlighted Scottish stinginess—which both Jews and Scots have been stereotyped as being. In fact, some of the jokes in the study were Jewish jokes converted into anti-Scottish jokes.[143] This study broadens superiority theory—in addition to just individuals seeing themselves as superior, members of a group see themselves as superior to another group that they share no affiliation whatsoever with.

---

142 Mark A. Ferguson and Thomas E. Ford, "Disparagement Humor: A Theoretical and Empirical Review of Psychoanalytic, Superiority, and Social Identity Theories," *International Journal of Humor Research* 21, no. 3 (September 1, 2008): 283–312.

143 H. A. Wolff, C. E. Smith, and H. A. Murray, "The psychology of humor," *Journal of Abnormal & Social Psychology* 28 (1934): 341-365

Naturally, the satisfaction gained from hearing or telling a disparagement joke is a sliding scale—for example, while some people may really like immigrants, others may only somewhat like immigrants, and others may feel neutral, so on and so forth. In a joke disparaging immigrants, the more positive a voter feels toward immigrants, the less amusement they will experience hearing such a joke, generally.

However, keep in mind that the individuals who are immigrants themselves will have a different reaction than, perhaps, a person whose best friend is a first-generation immigrant. In both cases, there will be a negative reaction, but they will vary in intensity. Nonetheless, both individuals identify or feel sympathy for immigrants, so they both will not find the joke humorous. On the other hand, someone living in rural Indiana with no connection to immigrants or the immigration system will generally feel more amusement at such a joke.

This concept is backed empirically—researchers have discovered that the appreciation of humor is correlated inversely with how much the individual likes the people made to be the butt of the joke.[144]

A third and somewhat related theory is social identity theory, within which social groups are viewed as competing—not only for material resources—but also for social recognition. After all, social acceptance can and will lead to more political resources and attention, overall leading to a better life for those groups with high social recognition. When a group is distinctively superior to another group in some way (e.g. the percentage

---

144 R. A. Martin, *The Psychology of Humor*. (Burlington, MA: Elsevier Academic Press, 2007).

of individuals in prison, higher voter turnout), they can use disparagement humor to push other groups down. From this perspective, disparagement humor helps bolster social distinctiveness significantly. This theory goes a bit further, suggesting that people use disparagement humor in response to a threat to their social status. For instance, if majority groups feel threatened by the progress of LGBTQ+ individuals, they might make jokes portraying LGBTQ+ individuals as promiscuous and satanic, as people did in the late twentieth century.

No matter the theory, disparagement jokes are self-enforcing; that is, since they are typically only said around like-minded individuals, there is no one there to provide necessary pushback. Without pushback, negative consequences occur. Researchers have found that Canadians who were asked to recite humor that disparaged Newfoundlanders adopted a more negative view of Newfoundlanders (a similar result was shown about people telling lawyer jokes).[145] As a result, it appears that the mere act of telling disparaging jokes can have a negative effect upon the joke-teller's attitudes toward that group.

Other researchers have examined if hearing a disparagement joke impacts one's perception of that group. In one study, it was found that men who were exposed to sexist humor and found it more amusing reported greater tolerance of rape myths and violence against women. Additionally, exposure to sexist humor expands the bounds of appropriate conduct in a given context, creating a norm

---

145 Thomas E. Ford, Christopher J. Breeden, Emma C. O'Connor, and Noely C. Banos, "Jokes and Humor in Intergroup Relations," *Oxford Research Encyclopedia of Communication*, September 2017, 1–25.

How Jokes Can Give Hope to Our Fractured World

of tolerance for such atrocious behavior.[146] On a broader level, there is evidence that mere exposure to disparagement humor can foster discriminatory acts and behavior.

As University of Kansas researcher Bruce Hayes notes:

Often we think of humor as something that can defuse tension and make things more lighthearted. But this is a peculiar type of humor that does exactly the opposite. It condones violence. It incites violence because the butt of the joke is the other, the enemy. It's a form of dehumanization. It's the same thing that we find with racist jokes and sexist jokes. It's only funny if you're in on it, and you're not the object of it.[147]

Aside from immigration—a pressing international issue—imagine how this looks in an international perspective. In war, when jokes are made about the enemy, the norms of war get pushed further and further back until they disappear entirely. If we allow jokes to permeate into our culture about our enemies abroad, especially when we have no direct way of empathizing with them, then we are willing to tolerate more atrocious behavior against them. On another, perhaps more terrifying level, individuals making high-level decisions (including the one to go to war) exposed to these jokes are more likely to want to go to war. It's completely and absolutely terrifying to have come to this conclusion, but it is an important one, as we are beginning to see that not all jokes are good.

In the next chapter, we will go over how to defeat disparagement humor, but what we first need to understand

146 Nalyn Sriwattanakomen, "Who's Laughing Now? the Effects of Sexist and Rape Humor," *Psi Chi Journal of Psychological Research* 22, no. 2 (2017): 85–97.

147 "Cruel Jokes Presaged Civil War in Renaissance France," The University of Kansas, June 8, 2020.

is the pervasiveness of this humor. When I started to realize how much of comedy relies upon putting another, less powerful group down, it became difficult to watch several of my favorite comedians without recognizing it. But what this has also allowed me to do is evaluate my own humor—and the humor of others.

Take, for example, two candidates running for President. Both are invited to a whole host of speeches and debates, and to appear likable, they try to be funny (or they have dozens of speechwriters write jokes, which is probably more likely to be the case). What kinds of humor do they use? Do they dismiss their opponent and their opponent's supporters through humor?

On the international stage, we can analyze how world leaders joke, both with each other and through their public speeches. Humor tells us a lot about a person's intent, as we have seen throughout this book, and if one leader is "just joking" about hostile tensions between two countries, odds are there's a bit more there than a punchline. We need to understand that humor is not always good—and in the international system, it can be a precursor to violent events.

13

Poe's Law

As a fervent user and creator on TikTok—the mobile app that allows users to share videos of themselves up to sixty seconds long for the world to see—I get a lot of comments. I tend to post a lot of content about international relations, mathematics, and every now and then I post a video about being Jewish (such as being proud of Jewish children for never spoiling Santa for any of their friends in preschool). On one video, I had just shared the stunning mathematical fact that $1 + 2 + 3 + 4 + \ldots$ all the way up to infinity (every natural number summed together) is equal to $-1/12$. This mathematical oddity is commonly referred to as the Ramanujan Summation.

Within days, my video had racked up millions of views, hundreds of thousands of likes, and over seven thousand comments. But there is one comment that I will struggle to forget:

Commenter: this guy looks like someone punched him in the nose, it swelled up, then he recorded this video lol

A weird comment, but it hinted in a not-so-subtle way that my nose was freakishly large—a common anti-Semitic trope. The "Jewish Nose" dates back to the middle of the nineteenth century and has been used to shame and degrade Jewish individuals since then.

My family is no stranger to anti-Semitism. When my family came on boats to the United States, we had the last name Berbitski, a relatively common Jewish immigrant last name. However, when my grandfather and his brother applied to college with that last name, they were denied acceptance—but when they changed their last name of the application to Burton, they were admitted.

Upon reading that comment, I wondered if I was the next victim of my family to anti-Semitism; however, I wasn't entirely sure. It made no sense that this person was drawing on such classic anti-Semitic tropes for the purposes of commenting on a TikTok video. Naturally, I reached out to the commenter to see what was going on. The commenter responded, "chill, i was just joking bro."

The comment has since been deleted. But the response lives in my mind.

It was the "just joking" defense that we saw last chapter, but transformed into the digital world. When I did more research on this concept, I learned of an internet adage dubbed Poe's Law, which originates from a comment made by someone with the username "Nathan Poe" on a creationist forum: "Without a winking smiley or other blatant display of humor, it is utterly impossible to parody a Creationist in such a way that someone won't mistake for the genuine article."[148] Hence, Poe's Law came into existence.

---

148 Nathan Poe, "Big Contradictions in the Evolution Theory," Christian Forums, October 1, 2020.

How Jokes Can Give Hope to Our Fractured World

Plenty of examples make it clear that it's impossible to tell the difference between sarcasm and genuine belief—and thus many have observed that Poe's Law has grown to apply to many other concepts, far from its Creationist beginnings. There's now a Reddit page that is dedicated exclusively to instances where Poe's Law applies—users gather and debate various internet comments and messages that could be either intentionally ironic or genuine beliefs.

While initially benign, there is a way to take advantage of Poe's Law. Much like people using disparagement humor then quickly resorting to the "I was just joking" defense, people can take refuge in the ambiguity that Poe's Law offers from any sort of accusation.

I like to think of Poe's Law like a chess game between a grandmaster and an absolute novice—but the grandmaster has absolutely no idea who their opponent is (or in this case, isn't). Even though the novice is doing nothing more than shuffling pieces somewhat absentmindedly across the board, the grandmaster will think that their opponent has some grand and magnificent plan. Cue absolute confusion, where the grandmaster has no clue if they're being destroyed or doing remarkably well. Since they have no clue who is on the other side of our fictional chessboard, they don't know what their opponent is thinking.

Therein lies the biggest issue with the internet that Poe's Law gets right to the heart of—we have no clue what the person on the other side of the screen is thinking, if they are acting humorously or intentionally being prejudicial. As such, if we call out the prejudiced behavior, malicious actors can retreat back to the "I was just joking" defense, no different than the commenter on my TikTok video.

Breitbart, the alt-right publication, had a tech editor and self-proclaimed "provocateur" named Milo Yiannopoulos, who perhaps better than anyone else understands how to take advantage of the ambiguity that Poe's Law offers. While openly allowing for bigoted claims that allow and, in many cases, proclaim racist and homophobic beliefs, Yiannopoulos makes the claim that "Are [the alt-right] actually bigots? No more than death metal devotees in the '80s were actually Satanists. For them, it's simply a means to fluster their grandparents."[149]

The best example I could find regarding Poe's Law comes from the far-right commentator Steven Crowder, who sells a shirt with the Cuban socialist Che Guevara with a stereotypically gay "limp wrist pose," and the text "SOCIALISM IS FOR F*GS," although where I placed an *, Crowder placed a little fig leaf.[150] Anyone reading the shirt would read the last word as a homophobic slur; however, when questioned about it, anyone wearing the shirt (including Crowder himself) can respond by stating how Che Guevara was captured in La Higuera, which conveniently means "the fig tree."

The logic of using irony to mask bigoted behavior conveniently allows for far-right ideologies to make the claim that they aren't bigots, they're just being funny and ironic. When far-right leader Richard Spencer started a Nazi salute and chants of "Hail Trump!" after

149 Jason Wilson, "Hiding in Plain Sight: How the 'Alt-Right' Is Weaponizing Irony to Spread Fascism," *The Guardian*, May 23, 2017.

150 Steven Crower, Twitter Post, June 14, 2016, 7:12 a.m.

President Donald Trump's presidential win, Spencer laughed it off, calling it a tribute in "a spirit of irony and exuberance."[151]

In 2017, the Data & Society Institute released a report about how disinformation shapes US politics, dedicating a large percentage of this report to how far-right actors use internet humor to spread white supremacist values. Dr. Alice Marwick, one of the authors of the report, calls humor a tool. As she summarizes, "Irony has a strategic function. It allows people to disclaim a real commitment to far-right ideas while still espousing them."[152]

For those who might not "understand the joke," think of the ramifications. In fact, you don't have to think as much as remember Pizzagate, the conspiracy theory from 2016 about a pizza parlor—Comet Ping Pong, was the hub of a high-ranking Democratic child sex and human trafficking ring. While debunked by a wide range of organizations and individuals, many members of the far-right continued to spread this conspiracy under the guise of how funny it was. But some coming across this theory thought it was true, and proceeded to threaten the restaurant's employees and anyone else associated with the restaurant. The owner of Comet Ping Pong, James Alefantis, stated to reporters that "from this insane, fabricated conspiracy theory, we've come under constant assault. I've done nothing for days

---

151 Joshua Barajas, "Nazi Salutes 'Done in a Spirit of Irony and Exuberance,' Alt-Right Leader Says," Public Broadcasting Service, November 22, 2016.

152 Alice Marwick and Rebecca Lewis, "Media Manipulation and Disinformation Online," Data & Society, Data & Society Research Institute, May 15, 2017.

but try to clean this up and protect my staff and friends from being terrorized."[153]

But for Edgar Welch, on December 4, 2016, he decided to take matters into his own hands. He traveled from North Carolina to Washington, DC, arrived at the restaurant, and fired three shots from a rifle. He would later tell police that he was "self-investigating" the theory, and that without him, the children would be subject to torture. Because of people spreading "jokes," shots were fired.[154] Fortunately, no one was hurt, but Comet Ping Pong would be subject to another threat a few days later, and an arson attack a few months after that.[155]

We must find a way to defeat the ambiguity that Poe's Law offers. Fortunately, I think I've come up with a way to defeat it.

In the perfect world, we need a culture shift. We must consider that every joke can be divided into two parts: intent and impact. The intent is to always be funny, but these kinds of jokes rarely have such an impact. The meaning behind the "just joking" defense is that "if I didn't intend to hurt you, then the impact didn't occur."

The division of intention and impact is difficult, but it's not a new concept. The legal system has been rather effective at creating the separation between involuntary manslaughter and murder. Involuntary manslaughter is when a killing is unintentional and the result of

153 Cecilia Kang K, "Fake News Onslaught Targets Pizzeria as Nest of Child-Trafficking," *The New York Times*, November 22, 2016.

154 Fruzsina Eordogh, "With Pizzagate, Is Cybersteria The New Normal?" *Forbes Magazine*, December 8, 2016.

155 "Feds: Louisiana Man Caught Making New 'PizzaGate' Threat," *The Daily Beast*, April 11, 2017.

recklessness; murder is when the killing is intentional. In both situations, someone was killled, but for involuntary manslaughter cases, it was not the intent of the perpetrator to kill. Regardless, both involuntary manslaughter and murder receive penalties for their actions, even though a murderer receives a greater sentence.

If we apply this to the non-legal world, we begin to see the difference between a joke and a direct insult. Both have an impact on the listener, and as such, both should be severely frowned upon. In fact, like involuntary manslaughter, these jokes must be treated as an attack—sometimes a lesser one than a direct insult, but still an attack nonetheless. When this is applied to the international sphere, look no further than Renaissance France, where the Protestants and the Catholics engaged in religious and political combat. This 1500s version of a *Comedy Central Roast* had the Catholics joking about the Protestants letting women and common people have access to scripture and Protestants making fun of Catholic indulgences and saint worship.

These literal "fighting words" led to the increased burning of heretics and ultimately to the biggest massacre of the century in Europe, including nearly forty years of civil war between the two religious nations.[156] These kinds of jokes have quite literally caused wars, and it's easy to see how this rhetoric transfers into the modern Westphalian system. Ultimately, the international system (and humanity in general) must shift away from Poe's Law-esque jokes to prevent future conflicts.

156 "Cruel Jokes Presaged Civil War in Renaissance France," The University of Kansas, June 8, 2020.

I understand that this is not an insignificant undertaking—hence why the international culture shift occurs within our dream world. To start this shift, we must first recognize when such jokes are being made. When we hear jokes at the expense of someone (or at the expense of a marginalized group), we know that the said joke is simply bigotry disguised as humor.

Then comes the fun part: defeating the joke.

It's simple, really: ask the person making the joke to explain it to you.

It forces people to explain why their jokes are funny to them—thus causing them to confront any bigotry that the joke requires to be funny. Sometimes people will double down, exposing themselves as prejudiced (and preventing them from using the "just joking" excuse). Others will stammer and backtrack, realizing that what they said was not appropriate. Either way, a positive outcome occurs.

It will be awkward. You must live in the awkward space and let it happen. Be strong. Know that by beginning with such a simple question, we can get others to recognize when these jokes are being made. When we all recognize and stop such jokes in their tracks, we will prevent horrendous consequences from occurring.

14

Patching It All Up

———

"What's wrong with death, sir? What are we so mortally afraid of? Why can't we treat death with a certain amount of humanity and dignity, and decency, and God forbid, maybe even humor."[157]

Robin Williams proclaimed these thirty-three words as Patch Adams in the movie of the same name. In the scene, Patch Adams is defending himself from accusations that he has been practicing medicine without a license to a board of medical professionals that wish to expel him for doing just that. Patch Adams admits to not having a doctorate of medicine, but he defends the integrity of the medical profession with such vigor that the committee acquits him.

It is my second-favorite quote from that movie.

My favorite quote from the movie comes all but thirty seconds later, when Robin Williams simply states, "A doctor's mission should be not just to prevent death but to improve the quality of life [of the patient]."[158]

———

157 Tom Shadyac, Director, 1998, Patch Adams. Universal Pictures.

158 Ibid.

I think that a similar message should be shared for those of us with the gall to be interested in international affairs. Something along the lines of "an international affairs practitioner's mission is not just to prevent their country from conflict, but to improve the quality of life of those all around the world." It doesn't have the same ring to it, but let's take a moment to really think about what the international affairs system is.

There is a theory in international relations that the international political system is anarchic; that is, it is every country fighting for themselves. There is no supreme government, no overarching authority, and no superior power is there to enforce all of the international laws and treaties. The world is truly every country fighting.

Or is it?

The great international relations philosopher Alexander Wendt stated clearly and succinctly, "Anarchy is what states make of it."[159] I tend to agree.

It is my hope that as you've read this text, you've had fun. While many of the jokes may not have translated over to the written word as well as I would have liked, they serve a unique and important principle. I like to think that every one of you have at least smiled at one of the jokes (or at the very least breathed out of your nose a bit more abruptly once or twice). If that's the case—and I think it is—then you all have come from different walks of life, with different histories and different stories and different communities, but we all laughed at the jokes in this text.

159 Alexander Wendt, "Anarchy Is What States Make of It: the Social Construction of Power Politics," *International Organization* 46, no. 2 (1992): 391–425.

Even though many of us have never met, we all have the shared connection through humor. My question is, why does that have to be limited to this book?

We've seen how comedy and humor are used as coping mechanisms, resistance mechanisms, as mechanisms for change and even as ways to fight wars. But what was the common thread throughout all this book?

Hope.

It was humor that gave people hope when they were staring death right in the face. It was humor that gave people hope when they were facing oppressive regimes at every turn. And it was humor that gave diplomats and heads of state hope for a better future, one free of conflict.

And as mad as it makes me to say it, it was humor that allowed racists and conspiracy theorists the hope that there were others like them out there. When disparagement humor was accepted, it gave hope for those ridiculous and awful beliefs. But fortunately, we now know about Poe's Law, and even more importantly, we know how to separate the good humor from the bad humor. Because when we begin to ask questions about the intent of the humor, we begin to truly understand how we can separate the comedy from the bigotry.

It's not difficult to imagine a world where people joke more, particularly when dealing with the very real and very serious issues that the world of international politics presents. Every time I had an interview with someone in the realm of international affairs, I always asked them what their favorite joke was. It didn't matter if they were an expert in nuclear policy, or talking about Belarusian humor, or if they were an Icelandic diplomat—they all had a favorite joke, and in telling it to me, they put their humanity on display; they always laughed. And that's the thesis of this book: that humor reminds us of the humanity nested deep within us all. Tell a joke and you're human—to joke, is human. Don't, and we are doomed to lose our humanity, and in the process, we will destroy ourselves.

Acknowledgments

First and foremost, thank you. This book is nothing without readers, so I am eternally grateful for those like yourself. There are millions of activities you could do with your time, so I am thankful that you chose to spend it with my book in your hand.

To all those who listened to me ramble on and on about weird jokes or niche history stories, thank you. While I'm sure it was agonizing, it was incredibly helpful to crafting my argument. I would also like to acknowledge my family, who repeatedly and consistently checked in on me to make sure I was okay during late-night writing sessions. Special thanks to my grandmother for being just as dedicated to the publication of this book as I was—sometimes even more so.

To all those I have interviewed for this book, whether it be for your story, your thoughts, or your advice, thank you. There are far too many to list here, but if you've been willing to talk to me about this project and my ideas, thank you.

I would like to thank the team at New Degree Press for helping me bring this idea to life. This includes Eric

Koester, Brian Biles, Benay Stein, Jared Rasic, and anyone else who received frantic messages from me at strange hours of the night when I couldn't figure out how citations work. This includes all the other authors I've met along the way who have supported me in ways I never would have imagined, particularly Nicole Bianchi for her support. I would also like to give a special shout-out to Dr. Tasslyn Magnusson, who gave me the kick in the tuchus I needed to make sure this book was the best it could be.

Finally, thank you to all of you who preordered this book, which in turn helped me cover the upfront costs of such a project:

Abby Frank	Claire Mitchess
Adam Hamdan	Collin Cheng
Ali McSperrin	David Burton
Alisha Sehgal	Diana Mutz
Andrew Skurnik	Ellen Nathan
Anna Lenaker	Elliot V. West
Arunabh Sinha	Eric Koester
Ashley Cavuto	Felix Dey
Athena Clark	Gabriel Lopez
Aurora Emilie Solstad	Gary Stone
Beth Peyton	Giuliana Carrozza
Bob and Kathie Burton	Grace Hoffpauir
Brandon Reynolds	Hannah Culkin
Caroline Feldman	Holly Simon
Cassandra Cogan	Hugh Bromund
Charles Whitemer	Ingrid Wilder
Cindie Harp	Isabelle Chiu

JD Ferries-Rowe

Jordan Schoonover

Julia Hartnett

Julia Lovera

Julie O'Hara

Juzel Lloyd

Katie Turner

Katie Woodhouse

Keith Munro

Kyle Brun

Laura Burton

Matt Burton

L.S.

Maia Gokhale

Marilyn Brenner

McKenna Bieger

Meghann Cash

Mihika Kulkarni

Myrna Nelson

Natalie Orslene

Nicole Bianchi

Nina Raman

Parker Abrell

Peter Kondakov

Rachel Gilbert

Rebecca Hollister

Robin Turner Feinstein

Ruthu Josyla

Samantha Gildea

Samantha Lord

Sophia Long

Sophie Tafazzoli

Sufyan Saleem

Susan Nelson

Suzanne Brozowski

Tim Harkins

Victoria Russell

Vik Kapoor

Appendix

Character Flaws and Georgetown University

Kuhle, Barry X. "It's Funny Because It's True (Because It Evokes Our Evolved Psychology)." *Review of General Psychology* 16, no. 2 (June 1, 2012): 177–186. https://doi.org/10.1037/a0027912.

"Prominent Alumni—SFS—School of Foreign Service—Georgetown University." Georgetown University, December 11, 2020. https://sfs.georgetown.edu/mission/prominent-alumni/.

01—Conversations Between Stalin and Obama

Astapova, Anastasiya. "Why All Dictators Have Moustaches: Political Jokes in Contemporary Belarus." *Humor* 28, no. 1 (2015): 71–91. https://doi.org/10.1515/humor-2014-0142.

Jiang, Tonglin, Hao Li, and Yubo Hou. "Cultural Differences in Humor Perception, Usage, and Implications." *Fron-*

tiers in Psychology 10 (2019): 1–8. https://doi.org/10.3389/fpsyg.2019.00123.

Sauter, Disa A., Frank Eisner, Paul Ekman, and Sophie K. Scott. "Cross-Cultural Recognition of Basic Emotions through Nonverbal Emotional Vocalizations." Edited by Edward E. Smith. *Proceedings of the National Academy of Sciences of the United States of America* 107, no. 6 (February 9, 2010): 2408–12. https://doi.org/10.1073/pnas.0908239106.

02—Make Sure He's Dead

Shifman, Limor. "Humor in the Age of Digital Reproduction: Continuity and Change in Internet-Based Comic Texts." *International Journal of Communication* 1 (2007): 187–209. https://ijoc.org/index.php/ijoc/article/viewFile/11/34

Wiseman, Richard. "LaughLab: The Scientific Search for the World's Funniest Joke." LaughLab, October 3, 2002. http://www.laughlab.co.uk/home.html.

03—Taliban Bingo

Anderson, Benedict. *Imagined Communities: Reflections on the Origin and Spread of Nationalism.* London: Verso, 2016.

Brottman, Mikita. "What's So Funny About 9/11?" *The Chronicle of Higher Education*, February 12, 2012. https://www.chronicle.com/article/whats-so-funny-about-9-11/.

Carpenter, Whitney. "Laughter in a Time of Tragedy: Examining Humor during the Holocaust." *Denison Journal of Religion* 9 (2010): 12–25.

Ellis, Bill. "Making A Big Apple Crumble: The Role of Humor in Constructing a Global Response to Disaster." *New Directions in Folklore*, no. 6 (June 6, 2002): 35–80. https://doi.org/10.2307/j.ctt46nsgh.6.

Herzog, Rudolph, and Jefferson Chase. *Dead Funny: Telling Jokes in Hitler's Germany.* Brooklyn, NY, New York: Melville House, 2012.

Hess, Amanda. "Why Teenagers Love Making Jokes About 9/11." *Slate Magazine*, July 6, 2015. http://www.slate.com/articles/technology/users/2015/07/teenagers_and_9_11_trutherism_jokes_how_these_memes_became_a_phenomenon.html.

History.com Editors. "September 11 Attacks." History.com. A&E Television Networks, February 17, 2010. https://www.history.com/topics/21st-century/9-11-attacks#:~:text=Economic%20Impact,-The%209%2F11&text=New%20York%20City's%20economy%20alone,Center%20damage%20is%20%2460%20billion.

Kahn, William A. "To Wit: Humor and Applied Behavioral Science." *The Journal of Applied Behavioral Science* 26, no. 3 (August 1, 1990): 329–30. https://doi.org/10.1177/0021886390263006.

Kuipers, Giselinde. "'Where Was King Kong When We Needed Him?' Public Discourse, Digital Disaster Jokes, and the Functions of Laughter after 9/11." *The Journal of American Culture* 28, no. 1 (February 9, 2005): 70–84. https://doi.org/10.1111/j.1542-734X.2005.00155.x.

McClure, Max. "Stanford Psychologists Find That Jokes Help Us Cope with Horrifying Images." Stanford News Release.

Stanford University, August 1, 2011. https://news.stanford.edu/pr/2011/pr-humor-coping-horror-080111.html.

Obrdlik, Antonin J. "'Gallows Humor'-A Sociological Phenomenon." *American Journal of Sociology* 47, no. 5 (March 1942): 709–16.

Plumer, Brad. "Nine Facts about Terrorism in the United States since 9/11." *The Washington Post*, September 11, 2013. https://www.washingtonpost.com/news/wonk/wp/2013/09/11/nine-facts-about-terrorism-in-the-united-states-since-911/.

Post Staff Report. "Sept. 11 Attack Most Memorable TV Moment from Past 50 Years." *New York Post*, August 27, 2013. https://nypost.com/2012/07/11/sept-11-attack-most-memorable-tv-moment-from-past-50-years/.

"Remembering The Onion's 9/11 Issue: 'Everyone Thought This Would Be Our Last Issue in Print'." Yahoo! News, August 25, 2011. https://www.yahoo.com/news/blogs/cutline/remembering-onion-9-11-issue-everyone-thought-last-162024809.html?guce_referrer=aHR0cHM6Ly93d3cuZ29vZ2xlLmNvbVS8&guce_referrer_sig=AQAAANbKr2UdNrACRGKqONdQJ3wOjp7M_e9FyaxBkA46O4eCtUukgsoT2Ej3DwhFDfdkcxmfgLFyEmSfrQpP3gIFg4SKgASEHT5zfoJ3rlMrqaePzN7POGdl_iXDMfctH45nnoMQJs2w5zCQ7ez-Y9W-4fEsbNxTI53LhQ7MV0pxjjIYlhttps%3A%2F%2Fwww.theonion.com%2Famerican-life-turns-into-bad-jerry-bruckheimer-movie-1819566170&guccounter=2.

Simon, Scott. "Sexiest Man Alive Gets 'The Onion' Taken Seriously." NPR, December 1, 2012. https://www.npr.org/2012/12/01/166293306/the-onion-so-funny-it-makes-us-cry.

The Onion. "American Life Turns Into Bad Jerry Bruckheimer Movie." *The Onion*, October 18, 2017. https://www.theonion.com/american-life-turns-into-bad-jerry-bruckheimer-movie-1819566170.

Walker, Carolee. "America.gov—Telling America's Story—Five-Year 9/11 Remembrance Honors Victims from 90 Countries." America.gov, September 11, 2006. https://web.archive.org/web/20080516171333/http://www.america.gov/st/washfile-english/2006/September/20060911141954b-creklaw0.9791071.html.

04—Judas, You On?

Boykoff, Maxwell, and Beth Osnes. "A Laughing Matter? Confronting Climate Change through Humor." *Political Geography* 68 (2019): 154–63. https://doi.org/10.1016/j.polgeo.2018.09.006.

"Climate Change's Toll On Mental Health." American Psychological Association, March 29, 2017. American Psychological Association. https://www.apa.org/news/press/releases/2017/03/climate-mental-health.

COVID-19 Dashboard. Baltimore, Maryland: Johns Hopkins University, 2021.

Episode. *The Daily Show with Trevor Noah* 25, no. 54, January 28, 2020.

Osnes, Beth, Maxwell Boykoff, and Patrick Chandler. "Good-Natured Comedy to Enrich Climate Communication." *Comedy Studies* 10, no. 2 (June 3, 2019): 224–36. https://doi.org/10.1080/2040610x.2019.1623513.

Petzinger, Jill, and Marta Cooper. "There's a German Word People Use in Times of Despair, and It's as Apt Today as It Was in the 19th Century." *Quartz*, October 18, 2016. https://qz.com/811186/weltschmerz-theres-a-german-word-people-use-in-times-of-despair-and-its-as-apt-today-as-it-was-in-the-19th-century/.

Seth Meyers, "Trump Addresses the Nation on the Coronavirus Pandemic: A Closer Look," YouTube video, 16:35, March 12, 2020, https://www.youtube.com/watch?v=-SoZcjMWxm8.

Stephen Colbert, "The Big Story Tonight Is YOU—A Special "Social Distancing" Edition Of The Late Show," YouTube Video, 10:34, March 17, 2020, https://www.youtube.com/watch?v=BvJ1BuEtZE0.

"Summary for Policymakers of IPCC Special Report on Global Warming of 1.5°C Approved by Governments." The Intergovernmental Panel on Climate Change, October 8, 2018. United Nations. https://www.ipcc.ch/2018/10/08/summary-for-policymakers-of-ipcc-special-report-on-global-warming-of-1-5c-approved-by-governments/.

Unsubscribe Memes. 2020. "Calm down everyone." Facebook, March 23, 2020. https://www.facebook.com/Unsubscribe-Memes/photos/a.1649126995206628/2776161989169784/?-type=3&theater&ifg=1.

Williams, Alex. "It's OK to Find Humor in Some of This." *The New York Times*, April 22, 2020. https://www.nytimes.com/2020/04/22/style/coronavirus-humor.html.

05—German Apples

2004 State Parliament Results, *Tagesschau*, 2004. https://wahl. tagesschau.de/wahlen/2004-09-19-LT-DE-SN/index.shtml

Boyer, Dominic. "Simply the Best: Parody and Political Sincerity in Iceland." *American Ethnologist* 40, no. 2 (2013): 276–87. https://doi.org/10.1111/amet.12020.

Front Deutscher Äpfel. "Nachrichten Aus Dem Führerhauptquartier." Front Deutscher Äpfel, November 1, 2018. http://apfelfront.de/.

Front Deutscher Äpfel. "Thesen Über Satire Als Angewandten Punkrock." Front Deutscher Äpfel, January 31, 2015. http:// apfelfront.de/thesen-ueber-satire-als-angewandten-punk-rock/.

"Hate Groups Reach Record High." Southern Poverty Law Center, February 19, 2019. https://www.splcenter.org/ news/2019/02/19/hate-groups-reach-record-high.

Layde, David. "German City Came Up With Genius Way Of Handling Neo-Nazis." Nova.ie, August 21, 2019. https://www. nova.ie/german-city-came-up-with-genius-way-of-handling-neo-nazis-167897/.

Nelson, Soraya Sarhaddi. "Hungary's Satirical 'Two-Tailed Dog' Party Will Debut In Sunday Elections." NPR, April 7, 2018. https://www.npr.org/sections/parallels/2018/04/07/599928312/hungarys-satirical-two-tailed-dog-party-will-debut-in-sunday-elections.

Steglich, Florian. "Satire Gegen Rechtsradikale: Ein Apfel Für Die Nazis." Der Spiegel. Der Spiegel, May 2, 2006. https://www.spiegel.de/lebenundlernen/uni/satire-gegen-rechtsradikale-ein-apfel-fuer-die-nazis-a-414103.html.

"Ukraine Election: Comedian Zelensky Wins Presidency by Landslide." *BBC News*, April 22, 2019. https://www.bbc.com/news/world-europe-48007487.

"White Supremacists Step Up Off-Campus Propaganda Efforts in 2018." Anti-Defamation League, 2019. https://www.adl.org/resources/reports/white-supremacists-step-up-off-campus-propaganda-efforts-in-2018.

Zeller, Michael C. "How to Laugh Away the Far-Right: Lessons from Germany." openDemocracy, July 30, 2020. https://www.opendemocracy.net/en/countering-radical-right/how-laugh-away-far-right-lessons-germany/?fbclid=IwAR3kwFossSYXUKiJpGqK7lpy0mqnKLo-ZxrM3DfB2unh_gdopOC61SbL7Co.

06—The Political Humor Paradox

8:46. YouTube, 2020. https://www.youtube.com/watch?v=3tR6mKcBbT4&ab_channel=NetflixIsAJoke.

Carpenter, Whitney. "Laughter in a Time of Tragedy: Examining Humor during the Holocaust." *Denison Journal of Religion* 9 (2010): 12–25.

Garron, Taylor. "What's So Funny About Being Black?" *Vulture*, June 19, 2020. https://www.vulture.com/2020/06/whats-so-funny-about-being-black.html.

O'Flynn, Kevin. "Toys Cannot Hold Protest Because They Are Not Citizens of Russia, Officials Rule." *The Guardian*, February 15, 2012. https://www.theguardian.com/world/2012/feb/15/toys-protest-not-citizens-russia.

Obrdlik, Antonin J. "'Gallows Humor'-A Sociological Phenomenon." *American Journal of Sociology* 47, no. 5 (March 1942): 709–16.

Ostrower, Chaya. "Humor as a Defense Mechanism during the Holocaust." *Interpretation: A Journal of Bible and Theology* 69, no. 2 (March 23, 2015): 183–95. https://doi.org/10.1177/0020964314564830.

Popovic, Srdja. "How We Used Laughter to Topple a Dictator." *Slate Magazine*, February 6, 2015. https://slate.com/news-and-politics/2015/02/srdja-popovic-on-using-laughter-to-topple-slobodan-milosevic-the-power-of-laughtivism.html.

Quirk, Sophie. "Preaching to the Converted? How Political Comedy Matters." *Humor* 29, no. 2 (April 29, 2016): 243–60. https://doi.org/10.1515/humor-2015-0046.

Tamborine. Netflix, 2018. https://www.netflix.com/title/80167498.

Wiesel, Elie. *The Gates of the Forest*. New York, New York: Schocken Books, 1996.

07—Jon, Hasan, and John

Aakriti. Twitter Post. March 17, 2019, 7:48 a.m. https://twitter.com/aakriti1/status/1107247305332150272

Adato, Alison. "Anchor Astray." Earthlink.net, May 2000. https://web.archive.org/web/20050116002844/http://home.earthlink.net/~aladato/anchor.html.

Burton, Sarah J. "More than Entertainment: The Role of Satirical News in Dissent, Deliberation and Democracy." Thesis, The Pennsylvania State University Graduate School College of Communciations, 2010.

"Content Moderation and Free Speech." Episode. *Patriot Act with Hasan Minhaj* 1, no. 7. Netflix, December 2, 2018.

Dadlani, Vishal. Twitter Post. March 19, 2019, 12:51 a.m. https://twitter.com/vishaldadlani/status/1107867203985014786

"FIFA and the World Cup." Episode. *Last Week Tonight with John Oliver* 1, no. 6. HBO, June 8, 2014.

Gibbons-neff, Thomas. "American Military Apologizes for Booklet With Racially Offensive Language." *The New York Times*, November 1, 2018. https://www.nytimes.com/2018/11/01/world/middleeast/american-military-racist-language.html.

Haberman, Maggie. "Clinton Talks Gaza, Media Scrutiny." *POLITICO*, July 16, 2014. https://www.politico.com/story/2014/07/hillary-clinton-daily-show-gaza-media-scrutiny-108967.

"Hasan Minhaj Show: Hasan Minhaj Decided to Talk Indian Politics, and Twitter Can't Keep Calm." *The Economic Times*, March 19, 2019. https://economictimes.indiatimes.com/magazines/panache/hasan-minhaj-decided-to-talk-indian-politics-and-twitter-cant-keep-calm/articleshow/68474087.cms.

Haynos, Evan. "The Newseum's New 'Daily Show' Exhibit Reminds Us of Jon Stewart's Impact." *The Diamondback*, August 27, 2020. https://dbknews.com/2019/07/24/the-newseums-new-daily-show-exhibit-reminds-us-of-jon-stewarts-impact/.

"Indian Elections." Episode. *Patriot Act with Hasan Minhaj* 2, no. 6. Netflix, March 17, 2019.

Late Night with Seth Meyers, "Hasan Minhaj Was Barred from an Indian Political Rally That Trump Attended," YouTube video, 6:41, September 24, 2019, https://www.youtube.com/watchv=lUoNEnY6ASM&feature=youtu.be

Luckerson, Victor. "The John Oliver Effect: The HBO Host's Real-World Impact." *Time*, July 10, 2015. https://time.com/3674807/john-oliver-net-neutrality-civil-forfeiture-miss-america/.

Marshall, Andrew MacGregor. "Thailand's Military Government Thinks John Oliver Is a Threat to Its Monarchy." *VICE*, July 24, 2014. https://www.vice.com/en/article/59a4dx/thailands-military-government-thinks-john-oliver-is-a-threat-to-its-monarchy.

Mazza, Ed. "John Oliver's Hilariously Awkward Throwback Photo Will Give You Hope." *HuffPost*, February 10, 2020. https://www.huffpost.com/entry/john-oliver-awkward-throwback_n_5e40ed5dc5b6f1f57f145c93.

Minhaj, Hasan. Twitter Post. January 2, 2019, 2:04 p.m. https://twitter.com/hasanminhaj/status/1080540270092005379?lang=en.

"Money." Episode. *Last Week Tonight with John Oliver* 3, no. 15. HBO, June 12, 2016.

Omran, Ahmed Al. "Netflix Pulls Episode of Comedy Show in Saudi Arabia." *Financial Times*, January 1, 2019. https://www.ft.com/content/5121f014-0db8-11e9-a3aa-118c761d2745.

Paeste, Paeste, Zapanta and Zapanta v. Guam, Calvo, Mangloña and Camacho (United States Court of Appeals for the Ninth Circut August 26, 2015).

"Saudi Arabia." Episode. *Patriot Act with Hasan Minhaj* 1, no. 2. Netflix, October 28, 2018.

Toscano, Nick. "Tony Abbott Roasted by John Oliver on HBO Show Last Week Tonight." *The Sydney Morning Herald*, June 2, 2014. https://www.smh.com.au/politics/federal/tony-abbott-roasted-by-john-oliver-on-hbo-show-last-week-tonight-20140602-zrvl1.html.

"Voting Rights for US Territories." Episode. *Last Week Tonight with John Oliver* 2, no. 5. HBO, March 8, 2015.

"Why You Can't Talk about John Oliver in China." *BBC News*, June 21, 2018. https://www.bbc.com/news/world-asia-china-44557528.

Worland, Justin. "FIFA Corruption Arrests: What John Oliver Said About the Soccer Group." *Time*, May 27, 2015. https://time.com/3897612/john-oliver-fifa-corruption/.

08—Wagging the Dog

Baum, Matthew A. "Sex, Lies, and War: How Soft News Brings Foreign Policy to the Inattentive Public." *American Political Science Review* 96, no. 1 (March 2002): 91–109. https://doi.org/10.1017/S0003055402004252.

McDevitt, Caitlin. "'Will & Grace' Applaud Joe Biden." *POLIT-ICO*, May 7, 2012. https://www.politico.com/blogs/click/2012/05/will-grace-applaud-joe-biden-122612.

Young, Dannagal Goldthwaite. "The Privileged Role of the Late-Night Joke: Exploring Humor's Role in Disrupting Argument Scrutiny." *Media Psychology* 11, no. 1 (March 19, 2008): 119–42. https://doi.org/10.1080/15213260701837073. (https://doi.org/10.1080/15213260701837073)

Young, Dannagal Goldthwaite. "Theories and Effects of Political Humor: Discounting Cues, Gateways, and the Impact of Incongruities." *The Oxford Handbook of Political Communication*, 2014. https://doi.org/10.1093/oxfordhb/9780199793471.013.29.

09—How to Topple North Korea

Chaplin, Charles, N. Rau, and M. Rau. *My Father, Charlie Chaplin*. London: Panter, 1961.

Chaplin, Charles. *Charles Chaplin: My Autobiography*. London: The Bodley Head, 1964.

Chaplin, Charlie, and Charlie Chaplin. *The Great Dictator*, 1940.

Elkind, Peter. "Sony Pictures: Inside the Hack of the Century." *Fortune*, June 27, 2019. https://fortune.com/longform/sony-hack-part-1/. (https://fortune.com/longform/sony-hack-part-1/)

Engelhart, Katie. "Former North Korean Poet Laureate Says 'The Interview' Is As Explosive As a Real Bomb Being Dropped on Kim Jong-Un." *VICE*, January 2, 2015. https://www.vice.com/en/article/vbnagy/former-north-korean-poet-laureate-says-the-interview-is-as-explosive-as-a-real-bomb-being-dropped-on-kim-jong-un.

Moorehead, Kristina. "How Britain Fought Hitler with Humour." *BBC*, August 30, 2019. https://www.bbc.com/culture/article/20190829-how-britain-fought-hitler-with-humour.

Runcie, Charlotte. "How the BBC Tried to Beat Hitler with Humour—and Why It's so Nice to Hear Some of It in The Archers." The Telegraph. Telegraph Media Group, September 4, 2019. https://www.telegraph.co.uk/radio/what-to-listen-to/bbc-tried-beat-hitler-humour-nice-hear-archers/.

Taylor, Jennifer. "The 'Endsieg as Ever-Receding Goal. Literary Propaganda by Bruno Adler and Robert Lucas for BBC Radio." Essay. In *German-Speaking Exiles in Great Britain*. Amsterdam: Rodopi, 1999.

Vance, Jeffrey. *Chaplin: Genius of the Cinema*. New York, New York: Harry N. Abrams, 2003.

10—The North Korean Jokester

Willmott, Kevin, Director. 2004. *C.S.A.: The Confederate States of America*. Hodcarrier Films.

"Humour and Diplomacy." *Diplomat Magazine*, February 5, 2018. https://diplomatmagazine.com/humour-and-diplomacy/.

Joy, Nicki. Essay. In *What Winners Do To Win: The 7 Minutes a Day That Can Change Your Life*. Hoboken, NJ: John Wiley & Sons, 2003.

Macdonald, Dwight. *On Movies*. Englewood Cliffs, New Jersey: Da Capo Press, 1981.

Mehta, Harish C. "Fighting, Negotiating, Laughing: The Use of Humor in the Vietnam War." *The Historian* 74, no. 4 (January 10, 2012): 743–88. https://doi.org/10.1111/j.1540-6563.2012.00332.x.

Rubio, Alberto. "Sense of Humour Is an Indispensable Resource for Diplomats." The Diplomat in Spain, January 27, 2018. https://thediplomatinspain.com/en/2018/01/sense-of-humour-is-an-indispensable-resource-for-diplomats/.

Schmiel, Gene. "Humor in the Foreign Service: Not Necessarily an Oxymoron." *American Diplomacy*, April 1999. https://americandiplomacy.web.unc.edu/1999/04/humor-in-the-foreign-service-not-necessarily-an-oxymoron/.

11—Funny Guy

Carpenter, Dick M., Marjory J. Webster, and Chad K. Bowman. "White House Wit: How Presidents Use Humor as a Leadership Tool." *Presidential Studies Quarterly* 49, no. 1 (January 8, 2019): 23–55. https://doi.org/10.1111/psq.12492.

"Excerpts From Remarks by Clinton at His Post-Election News Conference." *The New York Times*, November 9, 1996. https://www.nytimes.com/1996/11/09/us/excerpts-from-remarks-by-clinton-at-his-post-election-news-conference.html.

Mankoff, Robert. "Lincoln's Smile." *The New Yorker*, June 19, 2017. https://www.newyorker.com/cartoons/bob-mankoff/lincolns-smile.

Moy, Patricia, Michael A. Xenos, and Verena K. Hess. "Priming Effects of Late-Night Comedy." *International Journal of Public Opinion Research* 18, no. 2 (July 22, 2005): 198–210. https://doi.org/10.1093/ijpor/edh092.

Office of the Federal Register, and Dwight D. Eisenhower, Public Papers of the Presidents of the United States § (1953).

"President Meets with Leaders of Kenya and Ethiopia." National Archives and Records Administration, December 5, 2002. https://georgewbush-whitehouse.archives.gov/news/releases/2002/12/text/20021205-2.html.

"Reverend Raphael Warnock: 'Get Ready' | Campaign 2020." *The Washington Post*, November 5, 2020. https://www.washingtonpost.com/video/politics/campaign-ads-2020/reverend-raphael-warnock-get-ready-campaign-2020/2020/11/05/00731660-e441-41be-aa94-838c69e069e2_video.html.

12 – The Most Dangerous Phrase

Allport, Gordon W. *The Nature of Prejudice*. Reading, MA: Addison-Wesley Pub. Co., 1979.

Aschheim, Steven E. *Brothers and Strangers: the East European Jew in German and Jewish Consciousness, 1800-1923*. Madison, WI: University of Wisconsin Press, 1982.

"Cruel Jokes Presaged Civil War in Renaissance France." The University of Kansas, June 8, 2020. https://news.ku.edu/2020/06/05/cruel-jokes-presaged-civil-war-renaissance-france.

Ewin, R.E. "Hobbes on Laughter." *The Philosophical Quarterly* 51, no. 202 (January 2001): 29–40. https://doi.org/10.1111/1467-9213.00212.

Ferguson, Mark A., and Thomas E. Ford. "Disparagement Humor: A Theoretical and Empirical Review of Psychoanalytic, Superiority, and Social Identity Theories." *International Journal of Humor Research* 21, no. 3 (September 1, 2008): 283–312. https://doi.org/10.1515/humor.2008.014.

Ford, Thomas E., Christopher J. Breeden, Emma C. O'Connor, and Noely C. Banos. "Jokes and Humor in Intergroup Relations." *Oxford Research Encyclopedia of Communication*, September 2017, 1–25. https://doi.org/10.1093/acrefore/9780190228613.013.431.

Freud, Sigmund, and James Strachey. *Jokes and Their Relation to the Unconscious: (1905)*. London: Vintage, 2001.

Martin, R. A. *The Psychology of Humor*. Burlington, MA: Elsevier Academic Press, 2007.

"Refugees." In The Holocaust Encyclopedia. Washington, D.C.: United States Holocaust Memorial Museum, n.d.

Shifman, Limor, and Elihu Katz. "Just Call Me Adonai: A Case Study of Ethnic Humor and Immigrant Assimilation." *American Sociological Review* 70 (October 2005): 843–59. https://doi.org/10.1177/000312240507000506.

Sriwattanakomen, Nalyn. "Who's Laughing Now? the Effects of Sexist and Rape Humor." *Psi Chi Journal of Psychological Research* 22, no. 2 (2017): 85–97. https://doi.org/10.24839/2325-7342.JN22.2.85.

Wolff, H. A., C. E. Smith, and H. A. Murray. "The psychology of humor." *Journal of Abnormal & Social Psychology* 28 (1934): 341-365.

13—Poe's Law

Barajas, Joshua. "Nazi Salutes 'Done in a Spirit of Irony and Exuberance,' Alt-Right Leader Says." Public Broadcasting Service, November 22, 2016. https://www.pbs.org/newshour/politics/white-nationalist.

Crowder, Steven. Twitter Post. June 14, 2016, 7:12 a.m. https://twitter.com/scrowder/status/742676198443122688.

"Cruel Jokes Presaged Civil War in Renaissance France." The University of Kansas, June 8, 2020. https://news.ku.edu/2020/06/05/cruel-jokes-presaged-civil-war-renaissance-france.

Eordogh, Fruzsina. "With Pizzagate, Is Cybersteria The New Normal?" *Forbes Magazine*, December 8, 2016. https://www.forbes.com/sites/fruzsinaeordogh/2016/12/07/with-pizzagate-is-cybersteria-the-new-normal/?sh=656d37032b68.

"Feds: Louisiana Man Caught Making New 'PizzaGate' Threat." *The Daily Beast*, April 11, 2017. https://www.thedailybeast.com/feds-louisiana-man-caught-making-new-pizzagate-threat.

Kang, Cecilia. "Fake News Onslaught Targets Pizzeria as Nest of Child-Trafficking." *The New York Times*, November 22, 2016. https://www.nytimes.com/2016/11/21/technology/fact-check-this-pizzeria-is-not-a-child-trafficking-site.html.

Marwick, Alice, and Rebecca Lewis. "Media Manipulation and Disinformation Online." Data & Society. Data & Society Research Institute, May 15, 2017. https://datasociety.net/

pubs/oh/DataAndSociety_MediaManipulationAndDisin-
formationOnline.pdf.

Poe, Nathan. "Big Contradictions in the Evolution Theory."
Christian Forums, October 1, 2020. https://www.chris-
tianforums.com/threads/big-contradictions-in-the-evo-
lution-theory.1962980/page-3#post-17606580.

Wilson, Jason. "Hiding in Plain Sight: How the 'Alt-Right' Is
Weaponizing Irony to Spread Fascism." *The Guardian*, May
23, 2017. https://www.theguardian.com/technology/2017/
may/23/alt-right-online-humor-as-a-weapon-facism.

14—Patching It All Up

Shadyac, Tom, Director. 1998. *Patch Adams*. Universal Pictures.

Wendt, Alexander. "Anarchy Is What States Make of It: the
Social Construction of Power Politics." *International Orga-
nization* 46, no. 2 (1992): 391–425. https://doi.org/10.1017/
S0020818300027764.

Made in the USA
Columbia, SC
11 May 2021